Here's a Faith
For You

*The people that walked in darkness
have seen a great light: they that dwell
in the land of the shadow of death,
upon them hath the light shined.*
—Isa. 9:2

Here's a Faith
For You

ROY M. PEARSON

ABINGDON-COKESBURY PRESS
New York   •   Nashville

HERE'S A FAITH FOR YOU

Library of Congress Catalog Card Number: 52-11312

SET UP, PRINTED, AND BOUND BY THE
PARTHENON PRESS, AT NASHVILLE,
TENNESSEE, UNITED STATES OF AMERICA

To my wife
RUTH

*whose patient love and loyal help
made this book possible*

Foreword

THIS book is intended for people who are troubled—troubled by God's apparent disregard of them, troubled by the lack of meaning in their daily lives, troubled by their seeming inability to alter the direction which the world is taking.

It is meant for people who are wondering—wondering whether the lives they live are really worth the effort, wondering why God does not answer their prayers, wondering what happens when they die.

It is written for people who are searching—searching for peace of mind, searching for knowledge of their real selves, searching for a faith sufficient for a world on the brink of doom, searching for a way to get started in that faith.

It is the purpose of this book to help people understand the meaning of the Christian gospel for their daily living, to eliminate some of their doubts and fears, and to free them from the hopelessness which often holds them frustrate. Starting in man's need, it strives to end in God's power. It seeks to shed light, to open doors, to tell good news.

7

Here's a Faith for You

Called into being by the specific needs of individuals to whom I minister, these pages have been planned with special thought of people facing problems or crises for which they are not spiritually prepared, men and women interested in a simple presentation of some of the basic affirmations of Christian belief, college students looking for a reasonable approach to a faith not exhausted by reason, pastors looking for a small volume to put into the hands of young people or adults who are considering church membership. The substance of these chapters has been tested in the laboratory of my own parish, and I record my gratitude to my fellow members of the Hancock Congregational Church, Lexington, Massachusetts, for the stimulation and encouragement of their comradeship with me in the church's ministry.

R. M. P.

Contents

The heavens shall pass away with a great noise, and the elements shall melt with fervent heat, the earth also and the works that are therein shall be burned up. . . . Nevertheless we, according to his promise, look for new heavens and a new earth, wherein dwelleth righteousness.
—II Pet. 3:10, 13

1

A Faith for These Times

THESE words from II Peter strike the ear as strangely pertinent today. One does not need to grant the writer the knowledge of atomic energy to say that what he prophesied has now become a present possibility, nor need one think of him as being nineteen hundred years beyond his time to find in his predictions one of the major problems which any faith confronts today. Like a thief in the night, this "day of the Lord" can truly come. The elements can melt with fervent heat, and with a great noise the heavens and earth can pass away from sight of man. And no faith is even worth the name unless, while girding man to build for the best, it also gives him strength to ride triumphant through the worst.

We serve no useful purpose by hiding our heads in the

11

sand today. These are not pretty times, and of the possibilities confronting us, many are as surely tragic as anything ever could be. Already large numbers of men and women are serving with the armed forces. More will be called, and some of them will not come back. Even as I write these words, no man can say what dread catastrophe will come before they can be read. World War III may already have started. The atomic bombing of American cities is not beyond the range of sober thought. Our lovely villages may be blasted by great warplanes flying high above us; and unless we find a better answer to our problems than we have found already, the earth may become again as once it was before—"without form, and void" and having only darkness "upon the face of the deep."

These things I do not say because I am more afraid of them than any other man would be. I do not think that I am. Nor do I say them in the wish to frighten or discourage. Already many people are bearing burdens greater than they should, and I long to lighten them, not increase them. I use these words simply in the effort to face with frankness precisely what it is that any faith must cope with, and to bring to light the utter emptiness of any faith which cannot give us victory in terms of life as we really know it today.

I believe that such a victory is possible. I believe that such a victory lies only in the faith and life to which we give the name of Christianity, and four main sections of that faith I set before you now.

A Faith for These Times

First: A God who can be thwarted but not defeated. Many people think about the world today as they would think about a runaway horse. The driver has been thrown, and the reins have been lost. It has got out of hand, and unless some fearless soul can hurl himself upon the charging beast and drag it to a stop, no man can say what havoc will be done. To the eyes of ordinary men those words paint a true picture of the state of the world in these times, but Christians cannot rest content in that interpretation. The world, they say, is not a horse but a ship. God is still in command of that ship, and all the strife of men is like a group of people locked up in one of the vessel's compartments. They can spend their time in hatred if they want to do so; they can fight each other; they can resort to torture, mutilation, and murder. But they cannot change the course of the ship, or keep the ship from reaching port and landing safely those who chose to spend their time in more constructive ways.

When God made us, he did not fashion us to be machines, but men. One of the inseparable attributes of men is freedom, and from freedom you cannot divorce the privilege of choosing the bad as well as the good, the wrong as well as the right, the foolish as well as the wise. It may be assumed that God could prevent most of the misery which we have found in the world, and that the reason for his inaction at this point is not a deficiency of power but a matter of purpose. God could do it; but he will not do it, and the reason why he will not is that such intervention would inescapably involve dragging man down from his place of glory and

13

honor, only a little lower than the angels, to the level of an electrical mixer in your kitchen, which goes or stops as you determine that it shall and operates at speeds which you ordain. Under God man is free, and in his freedom are at once his glory and his shame. He can go to heaven if he wants to, but he can also go to hell.

But however many people choose that latter course, they cannot pull God down to hell beside them. They can separate themselves from God's victory, but they cannot defeat his purpose for mankind or bring final disaster to the ones who seek to do God's will. For those lovely lines of Coventry Patmore's *"Magna est Veritas"* speak a truth which man should know beyond all doubt:

> Here, in this little Bay,
> Full of tumultuous life and great repose,
> Where, twice a day,
> The purposeless, glad ocean comes and goes,
> Under high cliffs, and far from the huge town,
> I sit me down.
> For want of me the world's course will not fail:
> When all its work is done, the lie shall rot;
> The truth is great, and shall prevail
> When none cares whether it prevail or not.

God can be hurt. God can be delayed. God can be thwarted. But God cannot be defeated. This is still our Father's world, and "though the wrong seems oft so strong," the Christian does not lose his steadiness, because he knows that "God is the Ruler yet." [1] Righteousness is at the helm. Power mans the engines. Love controls the destination.

[1] Maltbie D. Babcock, "This Is My Father's World."

14

Second: A world which is good but not the final good. To accuse Christianity of otherworldliness is to betray an ignorance of what Christianity really is. God so loved the world, John wrote, that he gave the world his only begotten Son, and in the course of his earthly existence Jesus showed no disposition to look down upon the things which God had made. He spoke with admiration about the lilies of the field and the birds of the air. He went often up the mountainside to find his solitude among the sights and sounds of open country. And so deep delight did he apparently derive from food and drink that his enemies reviled him with the taunt that he was a gluttonous man and a winebibber. From the Christian point of view, writes Arnold J. Toynbee, this world is not a spiritual exercise ground beyond the pale of the kingdom of God. It is a real province of the kingdom itself—one province only, and not the most important one, yet one which has the same absolute value as the rest, and one in which our spiritual action can be fully significant and worth while. This world is a good world, and it is a part of our Christian faith that in this world we should rejoice and be grateful. Lobster tails in melted butter, radios and phonographs, oil burners and deep freezers, forget-me-nots in gardens and roses lying thick along the wall, summer trips to California and ocean voyages to Europe—if we can have these things and not become imprisoned by them, if we can have them and not possess them through some injury or deprivation which we work upon our fellows, these things of the world are good, and we do nothing but despise God's handiwork if we do not enjoy them.

But today we are faced with the possibility that this good earth of ours will one day be no more. Indeed, you can go even further than this and call that possibility almost a certainty; for it seems to be the common prophecy of scientists that if the earth succeeds in escaping the man-made destruction of war, it cannot avoid that vast astronomical catastrophe by which at last it will be completely destroyed. To the Christian faith it does not matter very much whether the end of the world comes tomorrow morning or fifty billion years from now. In the light of the best knowledge which men can now assemble, the end of the world is sure, and any faith is less than adequate which thinks of life as limited by earth.

It is therefore a matter of great concern that through the centuries before our birth the Hebrew-Christian mind has never been content to rest within those boundaries. "God is our refuge and strength," the psalmist wrote of old. "Therefore will not we fear, though the earth be removed" (Ps. 46:1-2). Or think again about those words from II Peter: "The day of the Lord will come as a thief in the night. . . . The heavens shall pass away with a great noise, and the elements shall melt with fervent heat, the earth also and the works that are therein shall be burned up." But that is not the end, the ancient writer says, for he lets one sentence intervene and then goes on, "Nevertheless, we, according to his promise, look for new heavens and a new earth, wherein dwelleth righteousness."

Even the largest telescopes can see but little of this universe in which we live, and all that man now knows about that universe is like a grain of sand in a ton of coal. The trouble with men, it has been said, is that "their world is bounded by human horizons." It is a part of the Christian faith that God does not lose if he loses the world; and that being thwarted in the battle of earth, he is not defeated in the war of his ultimate purpose; and that having been deprived of the good which the earth undeniably is, mankind is not by that fact deprived of the greater good in whose quest the earth itself is no more than a means to an end.

Third: A human life which is in the world but not of the world. That is, of course, a corollary of the things which we have just been thinking of, but in a faith for these times there has to be specific place for such an affirmation as the one which Paul made when he said that "if the earthly tent we live in is destroyed, we have a building from God, a house not made with hands, eternal in the heavens" (II Cor. 5:1 R.S.V.). On October 2, 1847, Emily Dickinson wrote in her journal these words: "This P.M. the names of the professors of religion, those who have a hope and those who have not, were taken. I cannot tell you how solemn it was, as one after another class arose. I saw more than one weep as her name was put down *'no hope.'* " [2] That is where so many of us stand today. We have no living hope, and we have forgotten that if our Christian faith means anything, it means that life is not dependent on flesh, and that when "the earthly tent we live in is destroyed, we have a building

[2] George Frisbie Whicher, *This Was a Poet*, p. 71.

from God, a house not made with hands, eternal in the heavens."

Every man on earth has a body, and in that sense man is truly in the world; but that which gives to man his special stature under God is not his body but his soul, and the soul is not an earthly thing at all. Being in the world, man is not of the world, and when his fleshly home of life is destroyed, man himself is not killed but evicted. Beside the bed of a woman who was dying, the doctor whispered to her family, "I am afraid that this little lady is going down." But the little lady was not so sick as he had thought, and with her eyes still closed she firmly remarked, "I am not going anywhere just yet, and when I go, I am going up!" And that is the Christian faith! In his dramatic monologue Edwin Arlington Robinson puts these words into the mouth of John Brown, "I shall have more to say when I am dead." And that is the Christian faith! Death is a universal experience, and confronted by that experience, whether in ourselves or in those whom we love, whether on our bed at home or on some far-flung field of battle, man needs to understand that "though grief is inevitable, despair is unchristian." The years of God are throughout all generations, and he gives to man forever for the shaping of his soul. When we reach the end of earth, we have not reached the end. For, being in the world, we are not of the world. Our natural home is with God, and God is eternal.

And then fourth: A Christ who wore the guise of man, but in that guise revealed to man the life of God himself.

A Faith for These Times

I often hear it said that it does not greatly matter which church one belongs to. "All denominations are the same," a man will remark. "I could belong to any one of them." For the most part I can sympathize with such statements and be as grateful as anyone that our various denominations are approaching greater unity. But he who gives up faith in Christ gives up faith itself in any Christian meaning of the term. That Jesus was or was not God dependably incarnate in a human form is more a matter of fact than of opinion. Either he actually was or he actually was not; it cannot be both, and though men may disagree about it, in the sight of God the truth one way or the other is seen and known. And it makes a difference! For if he was not, then proclaiming that he was is a cruel trading on man's need; but if he was, then that fact is the greatest news the world has ever heard. For that would be the end of seeing through a glass and darkly, and at that point in history where Jesus lived on earth, we should be able to see as face to face, know beyond most doubt what God is really like, understand as heretofore we have not understood what God intends that we should do.

The Christian faith has reasons for believing that the Man of Nazareth was in very truth the One he said he was, and firmly rooted there, it offers men the shelter which it has bestowed upon the world through all the centuries since Jesus came. For if Jesus was indeed the Christ, then nothing else really matters. God cares, and God can! That is the word that Jesus brings us. We are not left alone in a world where nothing counts but the little lights that we can kindle and the feeble strength that we can muster. God loves us still, and to that love he adds his wisdom and his power. We cannot always understand him any more than we could always understand our parents when we were no more than children, but if Jesus Christ reveals him truly, then we can surely trust him. We do not have to lose hope. We do not have to be terrified. For he who raised his Son from death will raise us too from anything the world can do to us, and no loved one lost from us is truly lost, because he still is held within the life of the God who never dies.

A God who can be thwarted but not defeated, a world that is good but not the final good, a human life which is in the world but not of the world, a Christ who wore the guise of man but in that guise revealed to man the life of God himself—there you have a faith for these times; and for that faith Dwight J. Bradley's "Let Your Own Light Shine" provides a good embodiment:

> We hear it said that the lights have gone out, in Europe, in the world.
> Such a thing has happened many times before.
> It was dark in Bethlehem on a certain night.
>
> .   .   .   .
>
> The lights had gone out then, in Judea, in Rome.
> Yet it was bright enough to guide three wise men on their way towards truth.
> Bright enough to rouse the shepherds to the coming of a prince of peace,
> Bright enough to fill a cattle shed where human hope was born.
>
> .   .   .   .

A Faith for These Times

What if old lights have gone out? Kindle new ones
    everywhere.

.   .   .   .

Get out your lamp, your candle or your lantern.
Put it in the window. Or better still,

.   .   .   .

Take your own light with you and go outdoors into
    the world.
You will be surprised to find so many there ahead of
    you.
You may be even more surprised to find that God him-
    self is there with his newest and brightest star.[3]

[3] *Social Action*, December, 15, 1940.

Then said Jesus unto his disciples,
If any man will come after me, let
him deny himself, and take up his
cross, and follow me.—Matt. 16:24

2

A Way to Get Started

IT is probably true that with the rarest of exceptions every person in the average church on a Sunday morning is at least in name a Christian. The likelihood is also great, however, that in the sight of God our incarnation of the Christian life leaves much to be desired. In the realm of faith we believe but have to ask God's mercy on our unbelief, and in the areas of conduct we do the evil which we did not want to do and leave undone the good we planned to do. For many of us the real Christian life is like consummate skill in music or painting—a cause for admiration and even for awe, but not for actual achievement on our own. The sense of intimacy with God, the sure knowledge of what is right and what is wrong, the unswerving control over our impulses and our appetites, the peace of mind, the freedom from fear, the unquestioning sacrifice of self to purposes beyond the self—we often long for them, but they always seem high and lifted up, and fearing that we cannot attain them, we do not even try.

But the Christian life is like a hammer—no good if never used—and so I set before you as concretely as I can a way to get started in Christian living. Real Christian living, not just a reasonable facsimile thereof. The way of life which Jesus chose himself. The way of life to which large numbers of people stand already pledged by reason of their membership in the Christian church today.

There are two steps which every candidate for Christian living has to take, and the first is that of investigation. Who was Jesus anyway? How did he live and how did he die, and how was he raised again from the dead? What did he think and what did he say, and what did he do? What obligations did he lay upon his followers, and what teachings did he give them about God, about prayer, about love and truth and sacrifice?

Too much of what we think we know about the Christian life is only hearsay. Too much is the fruit of plain ignorance, false information, wishful thinking. For the most part, our knowledge of the Christian life has come from sources far removed from Christ himself. It has come from stories which our mothers told us long ago, from things which we remember from the Sunday schools of childhood, from the sermons of ministers, from the comments of friends, from the observation of the acts and attitudes of men and women whom we assume to be representatives of Christian faith and conduct. It would be strange if, thus transmitted, the Christian life were not sometimes misrepresented, and what a host of people call the Christian life is not that life at all but only a caricature of it, a parody of it, a perversion of it. You will see it assumed that the Christian life means keeping out of trouble, but that is a false assumption. You will find it believed that the Christian life is synonymous with going to church on Sunday and paying lip service to the church's creedal statements, but that is an erroneous belief. You will hear it asserted that you do not have to belong to the church to be a Christian, but there is little truth in that assertion.

It becomes apparent, therefore, that the primary need of anyone who wants to live the Christian life is that of finding out what the Christian life really is, and for that purpose we have no better sources than those found in the New Testament. Here are the principal records of Jesus' life and teachings. Here are the writings composed in closest proximity to Jesus' living presence. And if we want to stand as near him as we can, we shall not be content with the testimony of the twentieth century or the nineteenth or the eighteenth. We shall go back to the first century, and sitting at the feet of those who lived while he lived, we shall let them tell us what he thought and said and did. For such a pilgrimage in faith four things will be helpful, and no one of them is beyond the reach of almost anyone: (*a*) a copy of the Revised Standard Version of the New Testament, to make available the fruits of the best modern biblical scholarship in the work of translation; (*b*) such a book as the *Abingdon Bible Commentary*, to give needed information about dates and authors and difficult passages; (*c*) a time and place for quietness; and (*d*) a heart hungry for the living Christ.

Thus fortified, you are ready to launch yourself out in your great adventure, and I suggest that you start with the Gospel According to Mark. Written about A.D. 75, Mark is the earliest of all of the Gospels now extant, and it probably depends in good measure on information provided by the apostle Peter. Mark's style is not unlike that of the modern newspaper. His Greek is not always good Greek. And the likelihood is not great that he actually witnessed himself many of the incidents which he described. But here is the earliest preserved account of the life which you are setting out to study. So read it through, preferably in one sitting. Let Mark tell his story to you as he told it to the people of his own time, and think about that story as the record of a life which was really lived, of things which truly happened, of words which were actually spoken.

Then turn to the Sermon on the Mount as Matthew gives it in the fifth, sixth, and seventh chapters of his Gospel. Matthew wrote perhaps ten years after Mark. He leaned heavily on Mark for the framework of Jesus' life, but apparently he had available as well a goodly collection of Jesus' sayings, and in the Sermon on the Mount he gathers up the choicest of them for brief presentation. Read that sermon through from beginning to end at one time. Then go back and read it again. Read it slowly. Read it prayerfully. Read it in the thought that Jesus stands before you in the room as you read, intends that sermon for you your-self, preaches it straight to your heart and your soul. Read it in the awareness that this is the Christian life which Jesus is talking about, that this is the life which you are seeking yourself, that this is what it really means to be a Christian.

From Matthew turn next to the thirteenth chapter of the First Letter of Paul to the Corinthians. The way of Jesus is the way of love, and here is the best description man has ever written of the love which Jesus lived and taught. When Jesus spoke of loving your enemies or loving your neighbors as yourself, it was this love he had in mind, and when we speak about the Christian life today, this love embraces almost all of it.

Go back then and read the whole of Matthew. Then Luke, written about the same time but giving insights neither Mark nor Matthew gives. Then John, composed about the turn of the century, and attempting to interpret the meaning of Jesus in terms which educated men of the day could understand. And then finally the Acts of the Apostles, the record of the early church, the witness of the way the first disciples followed out the life which Jesus taught them.

You may want to read a modern book about Jesus, and if so, you will find help in Edgar J. Goodspeed's *A Life of Jesus*. You may want more information about Christian beliefs, and you will find it in Georgia Harkness' *Under-standing the Christian Faith*. And lest your new-found faith not be related to Christian life today, you will need to read regularly some of the outstanding religious magazines in the field of missions, social action, and general news and opinion.

At this point you may protest that I am imposing a rather considerable load of work upon you. I can only reply that you would certainly expect to do as much if you wanted to learn to play the piano, or speak French, or refinish furniture, or even enjoy canasta. I can only reply that the Christian life is either everything or nothing, and if a man is unwilling to undergo such a disciplined investigation of it as I have outlined here, he would do well to turn his back upon the Christian life completely. For he is beaten before he begins.

The second step which every candidate for Christian living has to take is that of commitment, and it cannot be stressed too strongly that the second step must be made at the same time as the first step. If you want to get a start in the Christian life, you have to investigate it, study it, find out what it really is. But at the same time you have to bury yourself in it, commit yourself to it, throw yourself behind it.

It is too seldom recognized that Christianity is the greatest gamble any man ever can make. There is nothing tame about the Christian life, nothing safe, nothing even reasonable in the ordinary interpretation of that word. Christianity involves betting your life on things but dimly seen. It means going out on a limb without being sure that the limb will not break. It means throwing yourself into the water without any proof that the water will bear you up. Christian faith is often thought of as an exercise in believing things which are not so, or at the very most a practice limited to what you think or wish or hope, but faith really moves not so much in the realm of belief as in the realm of action. "Faith," writes E. Stanley Jones, "is not believing in spite of evidence; it is acting in disregard of consequences."

Getting a start in the Christian life is one point where we cannot have our cake and eat it too. It is one point where we cannot keep one foot on the bank until we find out whether we can really swim. Some things every man knows about the Christian life before he ever embarks on such a course of investigation as I have outlined, and what he knows he must practice without any reservation or he may as well stop where he is. It has been rightly said: "The law of the Christian life is that obedience comes first and only afterwards its reward. Those who will not attempt to do God's will are not likely to know much about the power that is given to those who do it." Everybody wants peace of mind. Everybody wants happiness, security, contentment, hope. But these are the fruits of the Christian life, not the Christian life itself, and the only way to get your apple is to plant and prune your tree, to spray it for insects, and then to wait until the fruit has ripened on the limb. You simply cannot stand back from the Christian life and ask God to prove its worth before you accept it. The only proof of the Christian life is the Christian life itself, and if you want to get a start in it, the only way is to start.

So while you study the Christian life, you live the Christian life. What convictions you have you put into actual practice, and even where you doubt the wisdom of Christ's teachings, you live them out just the same. I wish that I could tell you that your life then would be sane and sensible, but I cannot. I wish that I could say that you then would be successful as the world interprets success, but I cannot. The fact is that anyone who takes his Christian faith seriously is probably in for a rough time. His commitment is "for better, for worse, for richer, for poorer, in sickness and in health," and once he gives his life to God in that manner, he will probably feel like the man who has just stepped into a roller coaster. He might have chosen not to enter the car at all, but once he has taken his seat and the car has started moving, he is in for ups and downs over which he has but little control. To get a real start in the Christian life you have to assume that the recorded words of Jesus represent God's plan for you. You have to obey those words without any stipulation as to what God will or will not let happen to you, and from the moment of that great commitment of your life you will have both a growing knowledge that the everlasting arms of God are underneath you and a frequent bewilderment about the reason why he sometimes lets you drop so far before he catches you.

What a life it is to which God calls us through those words of Jesus! It is a life of loving our enemies, doing good to those who hate us, blessing those who curse us, praying for those who despitefully use us. It is a life of not resisting evil, turning the other cheek, going the second mile. It is a life of prayer and more prayer, and then praying again and still praying. We are to put God's kingdom before anything else in all our lives—before the material goods of the world, before any selfish purpose of our own, before father or mother or son or daughter. We are to lose our lives, deny ourselves, search out some hard and bitter task which no one wants to do but still needs doing, transform that burden to a cross, and bear that cross until God lifts us from it on some Easter morning of our own. We are to take this good news God has given us in Christ, and we are to spread it, announce it, proclaim it.

These commands are not the whole of the Christian life, but they represent enough of it to let us see what is involved in this commitment I am speaking of and how far most Christians have fallen short of its challenge. But if we want to get a start in that life, these commands must be obeyed, and they must be obeyed not in the abstract but in the concrete. They must be obeyed in terms of the neighbor you hate, the competitor you fear, the other demands on your time which seem to crowd out any chance of doing what Christ appears to ask of you, your weariness, your doubts, your jealousies, the dirty pans in the kitchen sink and the noisy children in the yard and your longing for an old age without any worries about where the next meal is coming from. There is nothing to be gained through the attempt to deceive ourselves at this point. Short of these commands of Jesus we can live a good life, a kind life, a just life, a happy life; but we cannot live a Christian life.

And obeying these commands of Jesus, we shall not live an easy life.

When Frank Buchman first urged Loudon Hamilton to listen for God's instructions, Hamilton replied: "I have been accustomed to address God myself on occasion, . . . but that was only a one-way communication. If God were to speak to me as you suggest, I am not quite sure it would not be somewhat uncomfortable." And so it will be with this business of getting started in the Christian life. As God begins to make himself felt in our living, we shall find increasingly that it is a fearful thing to fall into his hands, a troublesome thing, a goading thing. But there simply is not any way out. If you want the assurances of the Christian life, the convictions of the Christian life, the satisfactions of the Christian life, you have no other choice than first to live the life whose fruits you seek.

In the comic strip "Pogo" the duck comes up one day to talk with Pogo as he fishes by the riverside.

"Howdy, Pogo!" he says. "Is you seed my cousin?"

"Yo' cousin?" asks Pogo.

"Yep," says the duck, "he's migratin' north—by kiddie car."

"A duck migratin' north by kiddie car?"

"Yep, he's feared to fly high—afeared he might fall off."

"Why doesn't he swim then?"

"He gets seasick."

And then Pogo passes judgment on the duck's strange

cousin. "When he decided to be a duck, he picked the wrong business."

That is what has happened to many people dabbling in the Christian faith today. They have picked the wrong business. The Christian faith is not a marble but a diamond, and for a diamond you cannot pay a marble's price. The road to the empty tomb lies straight across the hill called Calvary. If you want to follow Jesus, you have to take up your cross. If you want to find your life, you have to lose it.

Take the Highways
Leading Upward

A LARGE number of "Christians" are skeptical about the Christian faith. They joined the church when they were young; they have attended church services with some regularity; and they have always tried to live a decent, honest, and neighborly life. But the expected peace and strength and joy of the gospel still seem strangely absent from their lives, and so they are skeptical.

And then there is also a large group of people who say that they are not Christians, but that they would like to try to be if only they could have a little greater confidence in the possibility of achieving what they seek. They are wise enough to know that if the assumption of church membership gives a man the right to be called one of Christ's followers, there is more to being really Christian than mere assent to a man-made vow. But nobody seems willing or able to give them sure directions, and so they are skeptical.

But there are ways out of this skepticism. There are roads to faith and certainty. There are highways leading upward.

The first of them is private prayer. You may have read the reporter's account of the emaciated little seven-year-old boy who sat in a wooden shack on the edge of an Austrian displaced persons' camp in Salzburg. With his father, mother, and two younger sisters he had just escaped from Hungary, and having been trained in the People's Democratic School at Budapest, he knew the answer to most of the questions put to him.

"What is your name?" he was asked.

"Sandor," he replied.

"What did you learn about in school?"

"Everything. The cat, the cow, the dog, and the beasts."

"Who set Hungary free?"

"The Soviet soldiers and the party."

"What kind of party?"

"The greatest party: the Workers' Party."

"Do you know who Stalin is?"

"Stalin is the great leader of the Soviet people. He likes the Hungarian people, and he sent his soldiers to fight."

"Against whom?"

"Against the Americans and the British."

"What did you hear about Korea?"

"We learned that the American soldiers bomb and fight

34

there against the Soviets and the Koreans. The Koreans worked on their rich fields peacefully, but now they are very poor."

"Who will win?"

"The Soviet people. They are stronger than the Americans, and Stalin leads them."

"Do you know who God is?"

"I do not know yet."

There you have a parable of the intellectual and spiritual state of great groups of our own people today. They know the answer to every question but the most important one. It has been said that "religion is not a matter of man-made gods, but of God-made men," and even in the Christian churches we do not have many God-made men today. It has been said that "the mark of a saint is not perfection but consecration," that "a saint is not a man without faults, but a man who has given himself without reserve to God," and even in the Christian churches we do not have many men who have given themselves without reserve to God. It has been said that "men nowadays take time far more seriously than eternity," and it is one of the inescapable requirements of the Christian faith that men shall take eternity far more seriously than time.

A Christian minister is often asked for "proofs" of God, but the only proof conclusive to the doubting soul is prayer. For prayer is a "dip into acid." Prayer is daring to "read the text of the universe in the original." Prayer is not asking for things, begging for things, pleading for things.

Prayer is actual communion with the personal God. It is genuine fellowship with the author of the universe. It is abandoning the practice of the scribes, who spoke with the authority of somebody else, and assuming instead the example of Jesus, who spoke with the authority of his own direct experience, the authority of nights on the mountainside and days in the desert and long, long hours when his heart was open upward and his mind sought no other knowledge than the knowledge of his Father in heaven.

You may not believe it. You may not like it. And trying it, you may find the experience time-consuming, troublesome, and often seemingly unrewarding. But Christian prayer is inseparable from the full Christian life. Instead of asking why you have not found this life that overcomes the world, you may be one of those who ought first to ask themselves how long it has been since last they really prayed.

The second road to Christian life and action is the family. In the quest for Christian effectiveness and confidence many of us are like a general who has misjudged the course of a battle. He thinks that the decisive engagement is being fought at the right of his line, and there he concentrates his principal forces. But in fact the enemy is only feinting there and even now is launching his real attack far off to the left. Nels Ferré has written that "no one can improve the world drastically and with such speed as is now needed except God; and He, respecting our freedom, will not do so apart from our cooperation. Our fullest cooperation can come only through the community of prayer." The basic element in this community of prayer is the family, and this is where we need our strongest forces now.

I do not know why it is that many of us are so terribly afraid of sharing any religious experience with those we love best. I suppose it is in part a natural unwillingness to bare our deepest thoughts to anyone and in part a fear that knowing what we actually are, the family will find incredible what we tell God we really want to be. But whatever the reason for our reluctance, with the rarest of exceptions we shall not reach our full stature in the Christian life until we reach it in the company of those most near and dear to us. Something happens when the members of a family lift their hearts to God in prayer together, when each member takes his turn in voicing to God the deepest yearning of his soul for each of them and all of them. Something happens when the members of a family read the Bible together, when they discuss the Christian faith together, when they speak together of the life which God wants each of them to live. In his letter to his well-beloved brother Philemon, Paul sends his greeting to the "church in thy house," and that is what the Christian family ought itself to be. It ought to be a church in your own house— a worshiping church, a learning church, a serving church, a church whose members are together moving ever forward in the knowledge of God and the love of God.

You may not believe it. You may not like it. And trying it, you may find the experience at first embarrassing and even humiliating. But until we share what we prize most with those we love best, there is a closed gate in the pasture; and although we may find food elsewhere, it will not be the best food, or the most nourishing, or the most satisfying.

The third road is the church. Do you remember the counsel Jesus gave his twelve disciples when he sent them on their mission in his name? And have you ever thought about that counsel as also meant for you? The disciples, he said, were to cast out unclean spirits and to heal all manner of sickness and all manner of disease. As they went, they were to preach that the kingdom of heaven was at hand. They were to cleanse the lepers, raise the dead, cast out devils; and putting even father and mother in a place that was second to him, they were to take up their own crosses and follow in the way he himself walked.

I have no doubt that Jesus really stood in need of this help which he asked his disciples to give him. I have no doubt that his gospel would have ended with Joseph's garden if human hearts and hands had not picked it up and carried it forward. But in the back of Jesus' mind there must have been a corresponding concern for the disciples themselves; for it is one of the neglected facts of all spiritual experience that God does not flow in where he cannot flow out, and that damming your soul's outlet, you grow weeds at your soul's inlet.

Someone has said that a man who does not have the church for his mother cannot have God for his Father, and rightly understood, the statement is the truth. The gospel of Jesus Christ is good news, and good news was meant to be told. The church is the earthly fellowship of men and women who have taken upon themselves the blessed task of proclaiming the gospel; and offered the rewards of faithfulness, they face also the risks of betrayal. For failing to use for their fellows the food God placed in their keeping, they find their hoarded bread turned to stone, and lose the treasure which they might have kept by giving it away.

In this area you may already be conscious that something is happening in some of our churches. There is a phrase in one of our hymns which affirms that "new peoples are learning to pray," and that is really happening among the men and women of this nation. New people are learning to pray. New people are learning to search the Scriptures for God's will for them. New people are learning to talk about God with their fellow men, to ask them to join the band of Christ's disciples, to urge them to make the Christian life their own. Already you may have seen lay people taking responsibility for work which you always thought was only for the minister, and you may sometimes have been disturbed by what you saw. That would not, of course, be surprising. People have been compared to porcupines, and porcupines do not cause much trouble for one another if they just sit quietly ruminating on the problems of the universe. It is only when they start moving around that the quills of one sometimes get tangled up with the quills on another, but it can also be said that only when the porcupines start moving themselves do they move anything else. For the real Christian life is a life of preaching, teaching, healing, cleansing. It is a life of service and of sacrifice.

You may not believe it. You may not like it. And trying it, you may find it the hardest job you ever tackled on the earth. I cannot help it. If you want to live the Christian life, this is one part of it which you simply cannot cast aside; and asking someone why you have not found the expected rewards of your Christian living, you may be one of those who still have never tried Christian living.

The fourth road is your daily work. Unless a man can find in his daily work an outlet for his Christian faith, his Christian faith will soon become a stagnant thing, cut off from the rest of his life and becoming at last an area disdained and avoided. In the notes which he wrote for a law lecture delivered about July 1, 1850, Abraham Lincoln set down some stern advice. "Resolve to be honest at all events; and if in your own judgment you cannot be an honest lawyer, resolve to be honest without being a lawyer. Choose some other occupation rather than one in the choosing of which you do, in advance, consent to be a knave." No more than Lincoln himself would I subscribe to the belief that all lawyers must be knaves, but his counsel is sound. We have obligations to God which supersede all other obligations, and if our daily work cannot be reconciled with what we honestly believe to be God's will for us to do, it may well be that this is what prevents our further progress in the Christian life.

In St. Joseph, Missouri, a bakery salesman left a package of rolls on the seat of his truck, and when he came back, he found in their place a bundle of religious tracts. One does not have to condone the theft of the rolls to be able to say that this is the substitution which needs to be made in the motivation of large numbers of us. The Christian workman is as worthy of his hire as any other man, but he does not work for money. He does not work for prestige. He does not work for security. He works because he knows God in his own life, because he loves him, and because he wants to help him make the world in fact as God intended that the world should be.

I do not have any illusions about what may happen to a man when he substitutes the religious for the economic motive in his daily work. He may go on to greater success than he would otherwise ever have known, or he may see his income cut in half and be forced to move his family to less expensive housing. But this fact is no less irrelevant than the common explanation that people do not come to church because Sunday is their only day of rest or their only day to mow the lawn or wash the kitchen floor. James and John probably "took a beating" as fishermen when they left their nets and beached their boats to follow Jesus, but where would the church be now if they had put their selfishness above their faith? What would have happened to Christianity if all the Stephens of its early days had said they would gladly follow Christ if only people would stop stoning them? If only the lions were out of the picture, if only the gladiators would all stay home, if only Nero would not light his torches—how many times the early Christians must have felt like that about the fate that lay in wait for them! But in the end it did not matter. They still went on. And so must we if we really are in earnest when we say we want to live the Christian life today.

It is the surest essence of the Christian faith that a man "ought to obey God rather than men" (Acts 5:29), and nowhere more than in his daily work. To do so he may have to change his occupation, or he may only have to find new reasons for the work which he has always done. But in either case the consequence to self is not a major consequence. He is fighting a battle, and any soldier knows that in a battle he runs the risk of being wounded.

The Christian faith is a probing faith. It is a goading faith. It is an upsetting, disturbing, revolutionary faith. And if in the course of your seeking and searching you never have felt as if you had got hold of a comet, as if you were being whipped about the world by something over which you had not the slightest control, as if you were terrified to hold on and even more terrified to let go, then the likelihood is great that you have never really lived the Christian life at all—in your own heart, in your family, as a member of the Christian church, as a daily worker in the kingdom of God on earth. And men can scarcely hope to find fruit in their orchards when they have not even set out trees.

Thank God
You Feel Inadequate!

SOME time ago I chanced upon some words by Gerald Kennedy.

> Human life has within it the element of despair. . . . This despair is caused by a gap between what man is and what he knows he ought to be. We cannot escape the feeling that we were made for greatness, and we cannot escape the conviction that we fall far beneath that state. . . . The human situation has at the very heart of it an element of tragedy. We are all disappointed men.[1]

Over and over again those words have come back to my mind as I have talked with those in need of help. "I feel so inadequate," a mother may say. "I want to be a good parent, but I don't know how, and the more I try, the more I seem to fail." Or "I'm just not up to it," a man may

[1] Gerald Kennedy, *The Lion and the Lamb*, p. 151.

remark. "I want to live the full, abundant life of Christian faith, but I can't do it. I have no time to think or read, no time to be a good husband or father, no time to pray. I don't even have time to be a real person. All I have time for is keeping abreast of my job, and I'm not much good at that. I'm nothing but a machine!"

There is a mighty host of people who could voice their frequent thought in words like those of the vagrant priest in Marcel Schwob's *The Children's Crusade:* "I am like a locust, for I leap about here and there and make a great buzzing." That is all that many people ever find in their lives, and knowing that they were made for better things, they spend their days in discontent. They feel incomplete. They feel ineffective. They feel inadequate.

To people like that the Christian faith has certain things to say. For one thing, it says that they are not alone. Few people like to wear their hearts on their sleeves, and none but the maladjusted enjoy the public display of their inner confusions. The fact that your neighbor gives the appearance of utter self-confidence means absolutely nothing. He may think the same about you, and envy you as you do him, while both of you would be the wiser if you understood your common doubts and fears. Some people are by nature more assured than others, and your moods of despair may sometimes coincide with your neighbor's moments of joy. But everybody has his ups and downs of emotional well-being, and the fact that you are sometimes "down" proves nothing but your membership in the human family. It is one of the characteristics inseparable from man that he often feels inadequate.

In the second place, it needs to be said that feeling inadequate, you are not crazy. Indeed, the fact that you feel inadequate is probably one of the surest signs that you are sane. For it cannot be avoided that human beings not only frequently feel inadequate but always are inadequate.

The world is too big for us, too complicated, too far beyond the reach of our human understanding and competence and goodness. It has been said that "all too often a clear conscience is merely the result of a bad memory," and it can be said with equal truth that all too often a feeling of adequacy is only the consequence of ignorance. Man is at the mercy of everything from accidents to microbes, and any moment of any day his life on earth may be brought to an end by a virus too small for microscopic description, or by a speeding automobile in the hands of a drunkard. The good that we know, we do not have the goodness to do, and about the truth we do not know, the words of Franklin give the proper attitude. "As yet," he said, "the quantity of human knowledge bears no proportion to the quantity of human ignorance."

It is one of the most frightening aspects of human life that every hour of every day we are called upon to do things which we are neither wise enough nor good enough to do. No parent is wise enough or good enough to bring up his children. No doctor is wise enough or good enough to treat his patients. Lawyers, ministers, insurance men, bankers, teachers—we do not have the knowledge we need for what we have to do. We do not have the integrity. And yet we have to go on choosing alternatives, making decisions, taking steps.

No sane man can dodge the simple truth: It is not only that we feel inadequate; we also are inadequate. And if some stubborn soul still feels rebellious, let him think about the single fact of death. For death is the incontrovertible witness of man's incapacity to save himself. It is the final proof that man is incurably inadequate.

Third, we can all be more nearly adequate than we are. "The spiritual life cannot be valid," writes Nels Ferré, "if we read the newspaper more leisurely and readily than the good news of God." And there you have the root of much of our spiritual poverty today. For many people complain about an inadequacy for which they are themselves responsible and over which they are themselves in full control.

Agnes Sanford has a passage of importance here. She begins by saying that not even the early Christians quite succeeded in living up to Christ's high standard of love, and as bit by bit they departed from the way that Jesus walked, little by little the power of God faded away from them. Generation after generation passed, and the great day of the kingdom of God seemed farther and farther away.

For still His people were waiting for Him, not realizing that He was waiting for them. Farther and farther away became

Thank God You Feel Inadequate!

the actual carrying out of His projects. For as century after
century rolled by and the power of God dimmed out from
among men more and more, they placed the responsibility for
this dimming out on Him and not on themselves. There came
a time when the actual working out of God's power was
the exception rather than the rule, and men called it "a miracle."
And after that, there came an age so dark that even the last
resort of the sick, the sacrament, was looked upon as the
fore-runner of death and men expected the Bread of Life to pre-
pare them for death, never dreaming that it would restore
them to life.[2]

Private prayer and public worship, psychiatrist and doctor and pastor, fellowship and friends, schools and col-
leges, bookstores and libraries—the tools of help are at the
finger tips of every one of us, and it does no good to cry
out that we cannot drive in a nail with our bare hands
when countless people have long since been begging us to
take the hammers they have offered us. Some inadequacy
is inescapable, but some is not. We could all be much more
sufficient than we are.

In the fourth place, most of us are already much more
nearly adequate than we think we are. We are so accustomed to measure adequacy in terms of public acclaim
that we find it hard to scale it in terms of actual achievement. Who can measure the adequacy of Lincoln's mother?
Or the single sentence of a friend that turns a man from
hopelessness to hope? Or the quiet courage of a woman

[2] From *The Healing Light*, pp. 53-54. Used by permission of the
Macalester Park Publishing Co., publishers.

Here's a Faith for You

dying of cancer and never knowing how she stirs the hearts and souls of those who stop a moment at her bedside?

Rufus Jones used to like to trace the connection between Savonarola and Hugh Latimer.[3] Savonarola's preaching in Florence had a profound influence upon a young man named John Colet, and as a result of that influence Colet's life was completely changed. He went back to England and there came into close relationship with Erasmus, who had come to England on a visit, and Erasmus' life was deeply changed by Colet. Erasmus went to Cambridge University and there converted Thomas Bilney, and it was Thomas Bilney who brought about the transformation in the life of Hugh Latimer, the man who, being burned at the stake in Oxford, said to his companion in the fire: "Be of good comfort, Master Ridley, and play the man; we shall this day light such a candle by God's grace in England as I trust shall never be put out."

There are chain reactions in places other than in the realms of atomic energy, and it is one of the most needed and neglected disciplines of Christian faith neither to be excessively elated by seeming success nor sorely cast down by apparent failure. It is not results which God asks of his creatures: it is only faithfulness. Our proper function is that of obedience to God's commands. The consequences are in his department, not ours, and in the steady, humble, earnest doing of the best we know, we often accomplish much more than we ever dream that we do. For in the providence of God the widow's mite can be mighty.

[3] See *The Luminous Trail*, pp. 93-94.

48

Thank God You Feel Inadequate!

It is a strange quality of the human heart, this sense of inadequacy which troubles so many, and the fifth of the things which every man should know about it is the fact that it is nothing to be treated lightly. Strange itself, it leads to strange places, and we ought to be on guard against the pitfalls on the way.

The most arrogant people are often people most surely conscious of their own inadequacy. Insecurity within creates the need for defenses without, and when you find yourself irritable and angry and vengeful, the chance is great that you have also found yourself inadequate. Promiscuity in the sexual relationship is most often not a sign of physical vigor at all. It is an evidence of frustration and confusion and tension, and many a boy or girl called "over-sexed" is nothing but an individual who has suddenly found himself inadequate as a person, who hungers for affection and love, who needs to be recognized as a being worthy of someone's attention and regard. In its extreme form the sense of inadequacy can lead even to suicide, and if you find it building up its pressures deep within your being, you had better get some help with it. You may have a time bomb in you.

It is a strange quality of the human heart, this sense of inadequacy which troubles so many, and if it is true that it can be productive of great harm, it is also true that it can bring about great good. For a sense of weakness may be the widest door to strength.

It is an old, old insight of the Christian faith that it is

easier for a camel to go through the eye of a needle than for proud men to enter into the kingdom of heaven (Mark 10:25). It is an old, old insight of the Christian faith that "not many wise men after the flesh, not many mighty, . . . are called" (I Cor. 1:26). It is an old, old insight of the Christian faith that "God hath chosen the foolish things of the world to confound the wise; and God hath chosen the weak things of the world to confound the things which are mighty" (I Cor. 1:27). Among missionaries returning from India, it is a common observation that the only people who were ready in considerable numbers to listen to them and to use their services were those to whom the Hindus referred as "untouchable," and it is one of the principal problems of earth that "there have always been men in the world so clever that God could make little if any use of them. They could never do his work as he wanted it done, because they were so lost in admiration of their own."

It is the very idealism of men which involves them in guilt, writes William Ernest Hocking; and we need to remember that we would not feel inadequate at all if we did not have the seeds of strength within our hearts. The awareness of insufficiency is the first approach of God to a human life, and the sense of weakness can be the widest door to strength.

The final thing to be said about this feeling of inadequacy is what Paul once said so many years ago, "Our sufficiency is of God."

Our sufficiency has always been of God. Of ourselves

we are nothing. We did not create ourselves. We do not sustain ourselves. We cannot defend or save ourselves. And when our life on earth is done, there is nothing in ourselves to make us more than rotting flesh or wind-blown ash. It has been rightly said that for genuine wishful thinking we must turn not to the Christian but to the agnostic, who, "out of the night that covers" him, blusters about his own "unconquerable soul." The Christian has better sense than to make that mistake. He knows that he carries his treasure in earthen vessels. He knows that of himself he has no sufficiency at all. But he knows too that he "can do all things through Christ which strengtheneth" him (Phil. 4:13). He knows that though with men his task on earth is not possible, with God all things are possible. He knows that his weakness is no obstacle to God's power, that God's grace is sufficient for all his needs, and that God's strength is made perfect in weakness.

And so it is that by his very weakness he is made strong, and out of his own sense of inadequacy he draws the confidence to overcome the world. For he knows that while the Christian faith does not affirm that man is adequate, it does affirm that God is adequate.

5

*We are troubled on every side, yet
not distressed; we are perplexed, but
not in despair.* —II Cor. 4:8

If It's Peace of
Mind You Want

SOMEDAY I shall go back to Vermont. Someday I shall
stand once more upon a hilltop there and be again as
once I was. Many years have slipped away since last
I stood there, but still I think about that lovely hill, and
often in the times of strain grow hungry for the hours I
spent upon it long ago, I need but close my eyes to see it
on a summer evening when, with supper over, I had walked
for seven miles up the little road from St. Johnsbury to
North Danville and climbed its slopes to watch the sun go
down. There was only one tree on its summit, and standing
at its base, you looked out over all the countryside around
you. On one side you saw the rolling horizons of the great
Green Mountains, brooding now on the valleys beneath them
and casting their shadows on the miles which they sheltered.
Across all of the east were the purple peaks of New Hamp-

shire, and sometimes when the night was clear, you thought that you could name the Presidents as they sat there with their heads above the dark. On the hill to the north the cows were in their pasture for the night, and southward across the valley the rows of white markers caught the last rays of the sun in the village cemetery. Now and then you could hear the distant bark of a dog in a farmyard, or the dull clonk of a bell from a cow on the hill, or the faint sounds of children at play in the tiny hamlet far below. But for the most part there was only quiet up there on the hilltop, and in the stillness you heard nothing at all. You could be at rest. You could be at peace.

It is such a state of mind which many of us seek today and seek in vain. We are sick of the tumult in the world around us, but in even greater degree we are sick of the tumult in the world within us. We are sick of it in the sense that we have had enough of it and would like to be rid of it, but we are sick of it too in the sense that it is a real illness which has laid us low. For he speaks needed wisdom who points out that the hunger for peace of mind is a clear sign of "the sickness of our time."

Whenever a generation talks long and anxiously about a philosophy of life, you may be sure it does not have one that works. . . . We are not worried about our health until we are sick; we are not concerned about happiness except when we are bored; we are not anxious for the good life until we are overwhelmed with the evil of our present life.

So it is with us today. We do not have peace of mind, and we want it. Because we want it, we reveal the sickness which has robbed us of it; and because we are sick, we need to find a cure for that sickness.

We are, however, Christians; and we do no more than waste our time if we do not bring to the search for peace of mind the basic insights of our Christian faith. In doing so, we face at once two warning signs which we cannot wisely disregard.

For one thing, Christians ought never to be guilty of seeking peace of mind as an end in itself. From the Christian point of view peace of mind is like happiness. It can sometimes be worthily sought as a means to an end beyond it: you try to set your own life in order for the sake of your effectiveness as a father, a storekeeper, a churchman. But when it really comes to you, you always find it in the category of an incidental by-product: you obeyed God's command for your life, and in losing your life in some unselfish enterprise, you suddenly awoke to see that you had found it.

The great temptation in the quest for peace of mind is to think of God as a vast vending machine. We take our little prayers, our Bible readings, church attendance, or other devotional disciplines, and thrusting them into God like nickles in a coin slot, we wait for him to give us what we want. And we fail to understand that the same rule applies to God as to every other person. Like the human creatures he has made, God is not a thing and can never rightly be regarded as a means to some greater end. God is an end in himself, and if we ever hope to know him as he truly is, he must be loved for his own sake, not for the sake of the things he can give us. For toadying to God in the hope that he will give you peace of mind is no more honorable than putting an apple on the teacher's desk in quest of good marks, or being nice to your grandmother in hope of her yacht.

Christians know that they were not put upon the earth to seek peace of mind, and that often the best way to lose it is to try to find it. We were put upon the earth to know God, to love him, and to share with him the burdens and the joys of his creation; and seeking God's kingdom first, we find that the other things are added. But they come not because we won them or even directly sought them: they come because God freely gives them.

The second warning in the search for peace of mind is simply this: We are running down a blind alley if we mean by peace of mind unruffled happiness, undisturbed contentment, uninterrupted pleasure. The ordinary pagan, of course, has the right to seek such freedom from distraction. The likelihood is great that he will never find it; for it is highly probable that the only persons capable of such achievement today are the mentally deranged. But still the pagan can go on looking for it, and no one has the right to tell him he must stop. The Christian, on the other hand, cannot even start the search at all. He knows that he was not made to be a vegetable. He knows that few of the really great men of the world have ever been peaceful in the sense that they were wholly at ease with themselves or with the world around them. But most of all, he knows that he is his brother's keeper, and even if the circumstances of his own life chance now to be good and pleasant altogether, he cannot keep his heart from the tragedy he knows about, whether it is on the other side of the world or only two houses from his own. In the commonly accepted meaning of the words, peace of mind is not always a sign of triumph but sometimes of failure, not an evidence of Christian character but of the absence of it. My dog is not worried about war, but that is one of the things which makes him a dog, not a human being. People are capable of suffering, from which animals are wholly free, and there is a large measure of that suffering which simply has to be accepted as one of the prices of our humanity. To be troubled by the state of the world today need not mean that you are crazy: it may be one of the surest possible indications that you are sane.

Yet there is a difference between being "troubled" in the Christian sense, and being "troubled" in the sense that one becomes neurotic. There is a peace of mind which Christian people have or ought to have. They need to recognize it when it comes to them, and they ought to find in it that confidence which the world can neither give nor take away.

In terms of the sea real peace of mind means knowing that though your ship is beaten and tossed about, and though your sails are torn and your decks awash, and though the storm swells and the land is far, your vessel will still reach port and the deed it was meant to do be done. In terms of the air such peace of mind means being sure that though the fog is thick and the rain is hard, and though the night is dark and the mountains high, and though the way is blind and the field unseen, your plane will still land safely because it rides a beam which can be counted on to bring it home. And in terms of human experience such peace of mind means being now as Paul once was in speaking of the life which he had lived himself. "We are troubled on every side," he said, "yet not distressed; we are perplexed, but not in despair; persecuted, but not forsaken; cast down, but not destroyed."

Such peace is of course God's peace, and stands upon the confidence that God, who made the world in the beginning, still has the final word about what happens to the world in the end. "If," writes Rufus Jones, "we could arrive at the conviction that the black squares in our checkerboard world are on a white background, and not vice versa, we could tackle our difficult tasks with courage and hope." Christians have the faith that this is true, and out of that conviction comes the peace which passes understanding but yet has been embodied in the words our fathers spoke of old. Those words, for example, from Deuteronomy, where Moses is talking to his people. "When thou goest out to battle against thine enemies," he says, "and seest horses, and chariots, and a people more than thou, be not afraid of them: for the Lord thy God is with thee" (Deut. 20:1). Those words from Joshua, where God is addressing the children of Israel after Moses' death. "Be strong and of a good courage," he tells them; "be not afraid, neither be thou dismayed: for the Lord thy God is with thee" (Josh. 1:9). Those words where the psalmist speaks his faith in language strangely pertinent today. "God," he says, "is our refuge and strength. . . . Therefore will not we fear though the earth be removed" (Ps. 46:1-2). Those words from Ps. 23, where the author speaks directly to the God who gives them meaning. "I will fear no evil," he prays, "for thou art with me." And then those great, grand words of Paul to the Romans: "I am persuaded, that neither death, nor life, nor angels, nor principalities, nor powers, nor things present, nor things to come, nor height, nor depth, nor any other creature, shall be able to separate us from the love of God, which is in Christ Jesus our Lord" (Rom. 8:38). From the Christian point of view peace of mind must ever be God's peace and be rooted firmly in the God who, though thwarted, cannot be defeated.

But peace of mind must also have its ties with earth, and of all of its earthly antecedents none is greater than the frank and intelligent acceptance of yourself as one of the planned children of the heavenly Father. You may be warped by your own errors or sins, and you may be twisted by the pressures of the world around you. But except for these perversions of your selfhood, you are as you are because God made you that way, and your life's fulfillment in general and your peace of mind in particular are both dependent on the way in which you take that self of yours and make of it what God meant that it should be. At this point your concern is not with any other man, but with yourself; and to your success or failure no other standards are applicable save the plan God had in mind in making you. So much of the world's agony is born of fruitless competition with our fellow men. So much of it rises out of the search for glory. So much of it comes from the refusal to accept our finitude. Would God we had the wisdom of the parable that Jesus told in speaking of the talents. No other man on earth can take your place on earth, or do the work which God has given you, or rival you in God's affection. If you happen to be a man of only one talent, you are that man because God made you so, and God will scarcely hold you responsible when you do not do the work of the man of two talents or five talents. For on the report cards of heaven the five-talent man who lives his life with only a 50 per cent effectiveness stands far below the one-talent man who lives his life with a 90 per cent effectiveness. We shall not have any lasting peace of mind until we let God love us as we are, until we stop taking a life which God intended as a hoe and trying to use it as a paint brush, until we understand that all God asks of any one of us is that he shall be himself as God meant that he should be.

And then there is the faith in life eternal, without which peace of mind will never reach the stature which it ought to have. If it is the purpose of our lives on earth to know God, to love him, and to serve him, then we can do that anywhere and at any time; and nothing which the world can do to us can wrench from us a life of meaning and value. And if our lives go on forever, then the need for haste is lifted from us. We are no longer pressed for time. We are no longer hurried, no longer harried. We have forever for the shaping of our souls, and we can take the time to shape them carefully and well. Where once we thought that we must run, now we can walk; and where once we thought that life would end before we had the chance to live a quarter of the days which we wanted to live, now we know that life will never end; and where once the tragedies of earth seemed irredeemable, now we wait in patience for the day when we shall be born anew beyond the present bondage of the body.

Then finally there is that ground for peace of mind in action undertaken in God's name and for God's sake. So much of our trouble today is the fruit of frustration. "If only I could do something!" we say to ourselves. "I watch the world in sober fact descending into hell, and my hands are tied. If only I could do something about it!" And yet the truth is less that we are helpless than that we will not take the avenues which still remain to us. Anyone can start building a better world any time he wants to do so. He can straighten out his own life, do a better job of rearing his children, volunteer for teaching in the church school, get out into the vast mission fields of his own town inhabited, as it probably is, by politely pagan men and women, just as lovable as any of the native peoples to whom we have long since sent foreign missionaries, but far more dangerous than they to the future welfare of the earth. Anyone who wants to build a better world can get into politics and make politics serve mankind, not grow fat upon it. He can work for the Red Cross, the Scouts, the Boy's Club, the hospitals. He will undertake these things in God's name and for God's sake, and in the doing of them he will know a peace of mind which otherwise would never come to him. He will find his frustration disappearing. New strength will flow into his soul, and being now actually engaged in combat with the enemy, he will lose the fears he had before he joined the battle. For you have to act as if you thought that God existed before he lets you see he really does.

Someday I shall go back to Vermont. Someday I shall stand once more upon a hilltop there and be again as once I was. There will be peace in my soul when I do, but peace which can be found nowhere save on the hilltops is not peace as Christians need to know that word today. Nor is it peace as God gives peace to those who love and serve him. God's peace is peace which passes understanding. It is peace which is not wrecked when the world is wrecked. It is peace as strong in valleys of the shadow as on mountains of transfiguration, and in those valleys unafraid because the Lord is ever nigh. God's peace is peace which knows that neither death nor life can separate a man from God's love, and hence that all of us can stand today where Paul once stood of old, and say again as he did then: "We are troubled on every side, yet not distressed; we are perplexed, but not in despair; persecuted, but not forsaken; cast down, but not destroyed" (II Cor. 4:8-9).

*Be not conformed to this world:
but be ye transformed by the renewing of your mind, that ye may prove
what is that good, and acceptable,
and perfect will of God.*
—Rom. 12:2

6

Don't Be
Pushed Around

NO one who has ever been in Lexington, Massachusetts,
could fail to be aware of its stature as "The Birthplace
of American Liberty"; and if you needed one sentence
to describe the attitude of those who earned the town that
distinction, you might say that they did not want to be
pushed around. On the evening of April 18, 1775, a de-
tachment of some seven hundred British grenadiers and
light infantrymen had set out from Boston under command
of Lieutenant Colonel Francis Smith of the Tenth Regiment,
and Major John Pitcairn of the Royal Marines. As the
minutemen stood on the green awaiting their coming, it
had been determined that they would not fire unless fired
upon, but neither would they let the British have free
rein in Lexington. They would not leave the town un-
protected. They would not allow its maltreatment. So in

the early morning light they stood there waiting for the redcoats—proud symbols of free people who cherished their freedom, who had minds of their own, who would not be pushed around.

Such has been this nation's mood through all the years since then, and on a deeper and an even more important level such the mood of Christians since the days of Jesus Christ himself.

Christians at their best have always been a nonconformist people, and surely that is what Paul had in mind in those words which he wrote to the Romans. "Be not conformed to this world," he counseled them, "but be ye transformed by the renewing of your mind, that ye may prove what is that good, and acceptable, and perfect will of God." Worldly men were often arrogant and haughty, but Christians were not to think of themselves more highly than they ought to think. It was the worldly way to strive with other men and take advantage of them, but Christians were to "be kindly affectioned one to another with brotherly love; in honor preferring one another." The world was frequently vengeful, but Christians were to "recompense to no man evil for evil," and if their enemy hungered, they were to feed him, and if he thirsted, they were to give him drink (Rom. 12:10, 17, 20).

Of course it is not hard to find the source of Paul's advice, for Jesus was himself the greatest nonconformist of them all. It was not the rich people who were fortunate, he said, but the poor; not the proud but the meek; not the persecutors but the persecuted. His followers were to bless those who cursed them and do good to those who hated them. They were to put God's will before their own, to sacrifice themselves for evildoers, to judge themselves not alone in terms of what they did but also in terms of what they wanted to do, to ask and trust that God would truly give. They took down every mold which they could find, his fellow countrymen and Roman overlords, but he did not fit any one of them. He was a radical completely. He was a revolutionary. He was a nonconformist. They tugged and squeezed and pressed and pulled, but still he did not fit the molds they used for other men. And so they killed him.

In the true line reaching back from now till then that strain of nonconformity has always played a major part. Peter and Paul, Stephen and James, Ignatius and Augustine, Wycliffe and Huss and Luther, John Robinson and Rauschenbusch and Gladden, Kagawa and Schweitzer and Laubach—they have not been copies; they have been originals. They have not been followers, they have been leaders. They have not been slaves; they have been rebels. We live a safe life, most of us today. We live a calm life, an ordered life, a life regarded by our fellows as both righteous and respectable. And in part because the need for nonconformity is often less apparent now than in the early days of Christian faith, the life which many of us live is a life far distant from the heritage from which we came. For our fathers were insurgents. Our fathers were insurrectionists.

But if the need for nonconformity is less apparent now than once it used to be, the need itself is no less real today than then. One could sympathize, for example, with the salesman in Sault Sainte Marie, Ontario, who paid a restaurant manager $1.10 to keep the jukebox quiet during his lunch. Or with the teen-age boy who was already to be confirmed when it became known that he did not believe an unbaptized infant would go to hell. His rector worked over him for some time and eventually became convinced that the boy had seen the light. But when the bishop laid his hands upon him in the confirmation ceremony and the boy gave assent to the statements of belief, under his breath and for God and his conscience he whispered, "Except infant damnation!"

Mark Twain once wrote, "We like a man to come right out and say what he thinks—if we agree with him." "I guess a lot of people are turning to religion these days," one woman remarked in the years of World War II. "I don't know but what it's a good thing. It's being advocated on the radio." And it was not many years ago that Clark Gable took off his shirt in "It Happened One Night," and revealing that he wore no undershirt, reduced the sales of men's underwear by 40 per cent, in a single year.

The radicals have become the reactionaries, and the rebels are the slaves. The fear of disapproval or laughter or failure, the patterns set by newspapers, magazines, and motion pictures, what other people are thinking or what other people are saying or what other people are doing— these are the cooky cutters of conformity, and pressed upon

the soft and yielding human dough, they shape us all alike.
But I prefer those words by Dean Alfange:

I do not choose to be a common man. It is my right to be
uncommon—if I can. I seek opportunity—not security. I do
not wish to be a kept citizen, humbled and dulled by having
the state look after me. I want to take the calculated risk; to
dream and to build, to fail and to succeed. I refuse to barter
incentive for a dole. I prefer the challenges of life to the
guaranteed existence; the thrill of fulfillment to the stale calm
of utopia. I will not trade freedom for beneficence nor my
dignity for a handout. I will never cower to any master nor
bend to any threat. It is my heritage to stand erect, proud and
unafraid; to think and act for myself, enjoy the benefit of my
creations and to face the world boldly and say, this I have
done. All this is what it means to be an American.[1]

In one sense that is also what it means to be a Christian;
for though the Christian emphasis on love has often left
upon the uninitiated the impression of weakness, it is, if
real, the surest courage and soundest strength. It declines to
be pressured, and treating with comparative unconcern the
incidental areas of the physical, it refuses to be pushed
around in the fundamental matters of the spiritual. Believing good will to be supremely important, the Christian does
not allow other men to set his own standards or permit his
offended pride to pull him from the heights he seeks to
climb; and so he takes instead the road that Edwin Mark-
ham counseled:

[1] Reprinted from *This Week* magazine by permission.

Here's a Faith for You

He drew a circle that shut me out—
Heretic, rebel, a thing to flout.
But Love and I had the wit to win:
We drew a circle that took him in! [2]

Having nothing but the greatest respect for the obvious contributions which psychological research has made and yet will make to the life of men on earth, the Christian still does not conform to the easy idea that all man needs for his salvation is to be "adjusted"; and he subscribes instead to Halford Luccock's caution that "the road to Vienna is not the road to Damascus. Psychology is a help to religious experience, but a poor substitute for it." Understanding fully the importance of the world in man's development, the Christian yet denies the common cult of geographical centrality and physical amplitude and time vastness; and he walks instead with him who said that "Carnegie Hall is a shrine of music even though it is not situated in the middle of the continent, and Rochester, Minnesota, is a shrine of medicine though it has but a few thousand inhabitants, and John Keats was a poet though he lived only twenty-six years."

Most people seem to think that force is the only way to deal with force, but Christians are not convinced. The country at large appears to be aware of no great moral issue in the spending of three quarters of our national budget for military purposes, but Christians know that God in-

[2] Reprinted by permission.

68

tended his creation for a higher end. The common standards of a job's attractiveness are its salary, its ease, and its prestige; but Christians think first about its effect upon others, its importance in the social structure, its place in God's plan. Large numbers of people consider nothing but their own "sophistication" in the alcohol they serve or accept at parties, but Christians will not put from mind the industry the alcohol supports, the social pattern it encourages, the way the money might better be spent. Calumniation of the Communists has become such a popular pastime that many of the noblest hopes of man are thrust from conversation lest suspicion fall upon us, but Christians here recall that this nation itself came to birth in travail and pain, that Jew and Negro, too, are people precious in God's sight, that free competition in the economic sphere has often been productive of misery and want and rank injustice.

"Be not conformed to this world," Paul told the Romans. Don't be cut into the conventional pattern. Don't be squeezed into the common mold. Don't be pressured. Don't be pushed around.

That counsel is as valid now as then, and just as needed also is the fundamental rock on which Paul reared this house of liberty for those who followed Christ. This was not anarchy which Paul was preaching. This was not the kind of self-expression which ends in nothing but chaos. "Be not conformed to this world," Paul said, "but be ye transformed by the renewing of your mind, that ye may prove

what is that good, and acceptable, and perfect will of God."
Christians could fear nothing in the world, but only because
they deeply feared something beyond the world—God.
Christians could refuse to obey men, but only because they
gave absolute allegiance to something greater than men—
God. Jesus' own ethics were the product of his metaphysics,
and his morality was the child of his religion. His revolutionary attitudes about men were saved from madness by
his conservative attitudes about God. He could break the
rules of earth because he kept the rules of heaven, and he
could scorn the kingdoms of the world because his kingdom did not belong to the world. For the individual himself the mere refusal to be pushed around can be just another name for haughtiness or conceit or arrogance, and for
society at large it can mean only disorder and confusion. But
not so with Jesus or with all who truly followed him
through all the centuries. On the level of men they were
nonconformist in the highest degree, but on the level of
God they were strictly conformist. Above everything else
in the world they sought to know the will of God for
their lives, and once they found it, they obeyed it. They
were too proud to be mastered by men but too sane to be
rebels with God. They had seen enough of their own frailty
to covet no longer the reputation of being self-made men,
and they longed for nothing so much as the right to say
truly that they were God-made men. They had traveled
down enough dead-end streets behind the little lights with
which men tried to illumine their own darkness, and now
they sought the highways where the hand of God was

70

pointing them. Now they had a fixed goal. Now they had a star to steer them by. Other men might pick up the costume jewelry, but they had the pearl of great price. Other men might have the world, but they had their souls. Other men might run the mile with great distinction, but for the marathon that stretched through all eternity they had the staying power that would never fail them.

Nobody likes to have the initiative taken out of his own hands. Nobody likes to be robbed of the freedom to live his own life as he feels that it ought to be lived. Nobody likes to be pushed around. But the roots of the real radical are never in himself or in his own self-will. They are in objective truth. They are in eternal justice. They are in God. And being firm in that connection, their seeming insecurity is nothing but illusion. They have learned in whatsoever state they are therein to be content. They know both how to be abased and how to abound. They can win success without presumption, and they can face defeat without despair. For they know that they can do all things through the Christlike God who gives them strength.

It is an interesting fact that John Quincy Adams was never quite sure that the voice of the people was the voice of God. "If the majority is fifty-one and the minority forty-nine," he asked, "is it certainly the voice of God? If tomorrow one should change, fifty against fifty, where is the voice of God? If two and the minority should become the majority, is the voice of God changed?"

As citizens of this nation we are rightly committed to

the proposition that the majority rules our government, but as Christians we have an even higher fealty. Our allegiance is to God. By prayer and by meditation, by thinking and by reading, by listening and by living—we seek to know God's will for us. Finding it, we do it; and conforming thus with that which God has asked of us, we have the right to nonconformity in anything which man demands in contradiction. We have no need for fear. We have no need for insecurity. We can decline to be pressured. We can refuse to be pushed around.

And he arose, and came to his fa-
ther. But when he was yet a great
way off, his father saw him, and had
compassion, and ran, and fell on his
neck, and kissed him.—Luke 15:20

7

God Takes Care
of His Own

IT was in 1902, and on the island of Martinique the vol-
cano of Mount Pelée blew off its head and covered the
town of Saint-Pierre with a deadly cloud of smoke and
lava. At that moment there was in the jail of the town a
criminal whose name was Auguste Ciparis, and when rescue
parties reached the jail four days after the eruption, they
found Auguste in the prison ruins. Out of thirty thousand
people in the town, he was the only one alive.

Events like that are major problems for the Christian
mind today. "Why doesn't God take care of his own?" we
ask. Little children died when Mount Pelée erupted. Old
men and women perished in that terrible catastrophe. Good
people, wise people, needed people—all of them were
killed. And who was left? Only Auguste Ciparis, the criminal confined in jail.

73

Here's a Faith for You

Why doesn't God take care of his own? Think of the multitudes of victims of the Nazi persecution. There were saints among them, and among them, too, uncounted thousands who, not saints, were yet a fine and faithful folk deserving any good which life could bring them. The Nazi armies were defeated, to be sure, but the innocent are dead. Or consider that mother in our neighborhood who died. She had three crippled boys in her home, and none could see them through as she could. The town and church are doing all they can to help those boys, but the mother still is dead. Cancer, arthritis, heart disease, infantile paralysis. Sometimes they strike the selfish and the cynical, but sometimes too they strike the noblemen of God. The saintly bear them with a dignity the selfish cannot imitate, but still their bodies are crippled, their talents are buried, their lives are cut off.

Sometime, somewhere each one of us confronts the problem which these facts present. If there is in truth a God almighty and eternal; if that God created us and gives us the strength by which we daily live; if he loves us and wills the best for us—then what in the world can God be thinking of today? Is he deaf? Is he blind? Is he asleep? Has he left the universe to hirelings and gone away on some vast cosmic holiday which, though long to us, is yet to him an insignificant occurrence in the timelessness of his creative purpose? "Why doesn't God take care of his own?" we ask. "Why does he let good people suffer? Why does he let bad people prosper?"

God Takes Care of His Own

Now before we say anything else, we ought to say that when we have gone as far as we can go in thinking out this problem, we still shall not be standing where we wish that we might stand. There is mystery which man will never penetrate, and when we fret about the multitude of things we do not fully comprehend, we often overlook the unavoidable distinction between the Creator and the created. God is high and lifted up. His ways are not our ways nor his thoughts our thoughts, and to expect that ever we could understand the whole of that which God has willed and done, is either to ascribe too little to God or to claim too much for ourselves. We are but a baby in his crib, and even if the father wanted to reveal to us the complicated world which he has known, he simply could not do so; for we do not have the background of experience to understand him. The universe is a big place, and we know nothing of it save the little that we know about the tiny speck of it which we call the earth. Eternity is a long time, and all the knowledge which we have of it is like the passing of a second in the span of a million years. We are upon the earth like the people who sometimes sit in the pews at the sides of our church in Lexington. They cannot see the altar. It is not their fault, and it is not their desire. It just happens that for the period of the service they have been put in such a place that the altar is out of their sight. Our being on the earth is such a vantage point for us. Some things we cannot see, and doubtless never shall while we are here; and if the searching mind is ever going to find a place of surer rest, it must sometimes take its stand upon the faith that many things which we can neither understand nor approve when viewed as we must view them, would seem both rational and good if we could see as God has seen.

Why doesn't God take care of his own? There is mystery behind that question which the mind of man will never penetrate, but that question holds as well a false assumption which no Christian ought to let himself accept. It is an easy thought that God's real children are the ones who love and serve him, and from there the step is but a short one to assume that God must feel particular responsibility for those who do the things he wants them to do. People who go to church ought to be successful in business. The man who loves his neighbor should never get cancer. The woman who rears her children in the Christian faith should not be killed in an airplane crash.

Without quite knowing that we do it, we sometimes think of God in terms which we despise when found among our fellow men. We make of God a kind of cosmic Teacher, and then we try to be the Teacher's pets. We bring him apples and flowers. We say nice things about him in his presence, and when we think that he is looking, we do what we know he wants us to do. And in return we expect to have him call us up before the class, put his proud hands on our heads, and tell the other boys and girls how wonderful we are.

Without quite knowing that we do it, we sometimes

think of God in terms which we despise when found among our fellow men. He is the Father of all of us, we say, and all of us are his children. So far, so good! But then behold the way our thinking goes. If people are "good," we want God to take special care of them—fend away disease, keep them out of accidents, spare them the loss of their loved ones, assure them steady jobs. But if people are "bad," that is another matter altogether; what happens to them is their own fault.

Suppose, however, that parents dealt with their children as we think that God should deal with his. You have, let us say, two sons. One of them is a source of steady satisfaction to you. He receives good marks in school, gets along well with other people, takes an active part in DeMolay, scouting, and the church. The second boy is just the opposite. He steals money from your desk, turns in false fire alarms, fights with other boys at school, throws rocks at a cat, ties tin cans on a dog's tail. How are you going to treat those boys? Give the first boy steak for his meals, the second boy bread and water? Take the first boy to the doctor the moment he is ill, but let the second boy fight it out as best he can? Call out a word of warning to the first boy when he does not see the automobile bearing down upon him, but be silent when the second boy is thus endangered? Of course you know the answer. Both boys are your boys. You love them both with equal love, and in so far as you can do so, you will give to each of them the same advantages, the same resources, the same protection. In fact, the likelihood is great that far from turning your back upon the boy in trouble and devoting all your time to the boy already well adjusted, you will spend a disproportionate amount of time in helping the one who clearly needs you most.

In wondering why God doesn't take care of his own we often take the attitude of the elder brother in the parable. He too was "good." He had wasted no substance in riotous living. He had stayed at home and worked as any son should work to help his father; and when his brother came home from the far country, he could not look with joy upon the welcome which his father gave the prodigal. "Why doesn't father take care of his own?" he said to himself, and he did not understand that this was just the thing his father was doing.

Every single creature on the earth is God's own child, and for God to discriminate between them in the basic conditions of their life on the earth would be unworthy even of a human parent. If there has to be disease, then it must be a peril common to the good and to the bad. If accidents have to occur, then Christian and non-Christian must share that risk together. If anyone has to be subject to the insecurities of economic status, then the saint must stand beneath that shadow with the sinner. For God loves each of us with equal love.

But that is not the end; for if all of us are God's own children, then we want to know why God does not take better care of all of us, why he permits so many accidents, so much pain, so much hardship. And the trouble with

78

that question is that many people asking it have overlooked the limitations God himself is forced to face. For even he cannot do the things which are by their very nature impossible of performance.

Most of our difficulties concerning the way God operates his universe fall into three main groups. The first of them is the product of the freedom God has given us, and few of us would willingly surrender that freedom. We want to be able to think for ourselves, and we want to be able to act for ourselves. We want to be able to decide for ourselves what we are going to do, where we plan to go, how we want to live. So far as our own freedom goes, we count God's gift of it to be an asset, not a liability, and it is only when another man's misuse of his liberty brings us pain or hardship that we even dream of blaming God for what at other times we call a blessing. But when my neighbor drives while drunk and kills my child, I ask God, "Why?" And frequently I fail to understand that God's hands are tied in such a tragedy. He could have made us puppets, but he chose to make us men; and once that choice was made, then even God could not avoid the consequences of that choice. He cannot give us our freedom and keep us in bondage at the same time; and if we have our freedom, then that freedom is for good or bad, and only we can make it good.

Then there are the questions about God's goodness which rise out of the order and the regularity of nature. For the most part we count that order and that regularity as a blessing. The alternation of the night and the day, the progression of the seasons, the way fire creates warmth and water satisfies thirst, the steady principles which make it possible for us to build an engine, fly an airplane, use electric stoves—these things, we say, are good. It is only when we happen to get in the way of those principles that we ask God, "Why?" Why was that good woman burned to death in her home? Why did that good man fall to his death from the top of that tower? And frequently we fail to understand that even God cannot so arrange it that we can have our cake and eat it too. Even he cannot create a universe at once disorderly and orderly, at once dependable and undependable.

And then there are the problems which occur because we live in the midst of a multitude of other people. For the most part we count this social network as a blessing, not as a curse. Doctors and hospitals, teachers and schools, miners, grocers, farmers, builders—where would we be if we could not depend upon the services our fellows render us within the one great human family? It is only when we suffer evil at the hands of other men that we lift to God the question, "Why?" Why was my son killed in the war? Why should my reputation be ruined by the lies that other people tell about me? Why should little girls be slain by sex maniacs? And frequently we fail to understand that even God cannot so place his children in the world that if our good helps our neighbor, our evil will not harm him. Even he cannot make us at the same time both a part of the social order and not a part of it.

Russell Dicks wrote these thoughtful words:

God Takes Care of His Own

One day I said to God, "I am sick of this world of sadness and destruction! Let me make a world wherein all things are perfect!" And God said, "Make a world that is perfect, and I will learn from you." And God gave me the power of creation and went away. And I made a world wherein all things were perfect and beautiful to behold. I made a world that was free from poverty and where every person had whatever he needed. I made cities that were great and beautiful, and countrysides that were free from the wild things of destruction. I made a world that was filled with abundance, and my people were free from envy and contention. . . . There were no physicians or nurses, for no one was ever ill or even died; there were no lawyers or judges, for no one ever disputed with another. There were no newspapers or magazines, for nothing unusual ever happened. No one needed to advertise, for no one needed anything. . . . There were no builders, nor those who care for cities and farms; there were no gardeners, for the entire countryside was like a lovely park.

And as I sat contemplating my world one day, God stood beside me. He said, "You have made a perfect world. It is lovely." "Yes," I said, "I have made a perfect world. Behold it!" God said, "You've made lovely fields and countrysides and beautiful cities." I said, "Yes, I have made them, and they are perfect." God said, "Where are your people? I hear not their laughter, nor their cries, their curses, nor their prayers." I said, "Come and see! You don't hear their curses nor their prayers for they don't contend with one another. You don't hear their cries, for they do not die. They do not fear the storms nor seasons. They have no fears!" And God walked with me through the country and the cities and the homes, and he said, "Your people do not smile. Your children do not laugh or cry." I said, "They do not cry because they are not hurt." God said, "They do not smile." I said, "No, they do not smile. They do not know either joy or sorrow." And I hung my head. God said, "They have no souls." I said, "No, they have no souls . . . They are dead bodies only." And God said, "Is that perfect?" And I said, "It is a tragic world—more sad than suffering and hurt." [1]

Why doesn't God take care of his own? The answer is that he does! He cannot give to finite minds the wisdom of the Infinite. He cannot make a petted brotherhood of those who claim to do his will a little better than their fellows do it. And he cannot give us at the same time the privilege of freedom and the security of bondage, a universe at once dependable and yet subject to unpredictable change, the blessings of society and the safety of isolation from society. But through the night and through the day, through youth and through age, through joy and through sorrow, through life and through death, God's love is with us as we go. He cannot force his love upon us; for we are his people, not his puppets. But to those who turn to him he gives the power of the peace which passes understanding and the life that overcomes the world. He gives the wisdom and the will to make all things work together for good. He gives the only assurance which in times like these is worthy of the name at all: the assurance that no blow of pain or depth of sorrow, no loss of health or death of loved ones, no circumstances of living or manner of dying, no tragedy of earth or cataclysm of the worlds beyond the earth, shall be able to separate us from his power, his care, his love.

[1] From "God and Suffering." Used by permission of the Associated Church Press.

8

For I am persuaded, that neither
death, nor life . . . shall be able to
separate us from the love of God,
which is in Christ Jesus our Lord.
                    —Rom. 8:38-39

Your Prayers
Are Answered

IN Pittsburgh a man admitted in court that he used to
beat his wife with some regularity, but he said that he
had long since given up the practice. Asked why he had
stopped, he gave a very simple answer. "I stopped," he said,
"When I found out that it wasn't doing any good."

That is what has happened to many people in their ex-
periments with prayer. They stopped praying because
prayer did not seem to do any good. They had prayed for a
new automobile, but they did not get it. They had prayed
for peace of mind, but still they felt distraught. They had
stood beside the bed of one they loved and asked that he
be spared, but even as they stood there praying, the loved
one slipped away to death. When you pick up the telephone
receiver, the operator says, "Number, please?" When you
meet a friend on the street, you say, "Hello, Jim!" and Jim

says "Hello!" in return. But when you pray, the only answer you seem to get is silence, and the greatest difficulty many people have with prayer is this apparent lack of response, this seeming ineffectiveness, this absence of assurance that the prayer has been heard and understood and adequately dealt with.

Yet in the deepest meaning of the words no honest prayer is ever left unanswered. "Can you tell me how to get to Rogers Avenue?" you ask a stranger on the street, and if he stalks away without reply, you think him oddly lacking in good manners. "Is it all right to park my car in front of this store?" you say to the policeman standing on the curb, and if he does no more than glare at you and go on talking with the pretty girl beside him, you take his number and report him for his insolence. Any decent individual will answer when you speak to him, and it would be unthinkable that God be found less courteous than man. It is the Christian faith that God is best revealed in Jesus Christ, and of the qualities which are distinctive of the Man of Nazareth, the clearest one is what we mean by words like love, understanding, sympathy, helpfulness, mercy. In that sense we say that God is Christlike, and if this is sober truth, then God answers prayer. He answers every prayer, and if it sometimes seems that he has turned his back upon our need, we do well to remember that two explanations are possible: that God's response was never made, or that it was not recognized. It is our custom to accept the first explanation, but we wrong God in doing so. God never leaves the suppliant outside the gate. He always answers prayer.

That fact is first in any thought of prayer, and when that fact has been understood, it becomes apparent that the real source of our difficulty is in the kind of answer which we think that we should get in prayer. For so frequently in prayer we are like a man who tries to use his hammer as a screw driver. The tool was not designed to be so used, and being turned to ends for which it has no suitability, it proves to be completely ineffective.

And so with prayer. Many years have passed since thinking people have tried to conceive God in their own image, and you would have to search awhile today to find adults whose God is thought of as a bushy-bearded Santa Claus. God, we say, is spirit. But man himself is a strange creature, compounded by God of both body and soul, and when he tries to enter into conversation with his Maker, he is apt to be confused. In such communication he will often rightly use his body; for he will sometimes bow his head, get down on his knees, fold his hands, close his eyes, or speak audible words. But he is likely to overlook the fact that if God is spirit, "those who worship him must worship in spirit" (John 4:24 R.S.V.), and he is prone to forget that since prayer is a spiritual engagement, the fruits of prayer may be sought with greater reason by the mind than by the eyes, by the soul than by the ears.

"Prayer," said Jeremy Taylor, "is the ascent of the mind to

God." "Prayer," said Augustine, "is not petitioning God for things; it is petitioning for God." And then there are those later words which set the truth in terms we understand today:

Even if science could demonstrate that prayer could never effect any kind of utilitarian results, still prayer on its loftier side would remain untouched, and persons of spiritual reach would go on praying as before. . . . Prayer, like faith, is itself the victory. The seeking is the finding. The wrestling is the blessing. It is no more a means to something else than love is. It is an end in itself. It is its own excuse for being.[1]

Christian prayer is not the effort to add to God's knowledge or to change God's mind. It is the experience of communion with God, of fellowship with him, of union with him. That is what prayer rightly is and all it seeks to be, and to ask of prayer more than this is like trying to eat broken glass when you might have steak, or like selling your son to buy a dog. To pray is consciously to be with God, and consciously to be with God is all the answer which the noblest prayer can rightly seek. For the five-year-old's rendering of the twenty-third psalm was wiser than he knew. "The Lord's my shepherd," he recited. "That's all I want."

But still the mind of man is not as God's, and still we ask of God specific things, and still he does not despise us

[1] Rufus Jones, *A Call to What Is Vital*, p. 139.

when we choose this lower level for our prayers. For even on this lower level God responds to every word which man addresses to him, and the real bewilderment of man is not that God refuses to reply, but that he does not always answer as we hoped he would.

In the minds of most people, having their prayers answered means getting what they want, hearing God say "Yes!" to them; and they do not seem to understand that sometimes God must answer "No!"

When you really stop to think about it, that is neither strange nor hard to understand. A parent often has to give that answer to his children. To live on nothing but desserts, never to go to public school or Sunday school, never to wash the hands or clean the teeth, to stay up all night watching television, to take the cat to bed with them and let the dog eat supper in the dining room—these are the prayers of countless children to their fathers and their mothers. Parents do not refuse to answer those prayers, but neither do they ordinarily reply to them with "Yes!" They have to say "No!" and often they are thought to be unfeeling when they do.

And so with prayer; for we have a low opinion of God if we do not recognize that the gap between his understanding and ours is at least as great as that between our own and our children's. We pray that we may have a sunny day for our picnic, but God says "No!" because he knows that wheat is needed more than picnics. We see the speeding car bear down upon the little child, and we pray that God will spare the child, but God says "No!" because he knows how much depends upon a world of regularity and order. We hate a neighbor down the street, and we pray that God will take him quickly to his final resting place, but God says "No!" because God sees the evil not only in our neighbor but also in ourselves, and cherishes alike for both of us the purpose of life, not of death.

"What discontent we would bring about in the world if all our prayers were answered," Longfellow once said. "When the Gods wish to punish us," said Oscar Wilde, "they answer our prayers." And then there are those words of Shakespeare in *Antony and Cleopatra*:

> We, ignorant of ourselves,
> Beg often our own harms, which the wise powers
> Deny us for our good; so find we profit
> By losing of our prayers.

Sometimes we pray in ignorance. Sometimes we try to make prayer a substitute for honest toil. And sometimes we so phrase our prayer that granting its form would involve denying its substance. To prayers such as these God answers "No!" But when he does, his motive is love, his end is our welfare, and his judgment is made in the light of omniscience.

Still further, sometimes God's answer is provisional. It is, again, the one which parents often give their children. Your son cannot have a shotgun like his daddy's now, but you will guide him toward such skill and carefulness that later years will bring him that right and privilege. Your daughter cannot stay out until midnight yet, but you will help her so to grow in wisdom and in grace that one day she will have the freedom which she longs to use today.

And so it is with God in prayer. Some things he does not give us when we ask for them because to do so lies beyond the range of present possibility. Even God, for example, cannot give you roses blooming in your garden two minutes after you decide you want them there. But give him time and your co-operation, and next June the roses will be blossoming beside your window. Even God cannot transform your selfishness to love before you say "Jack Robinson." But lift your heart to him in daily supplication; obey his will as he reveals that will to you; and sooner than you think, the evil will diminish, and love will have its place.

Some things, too, God does not give us when we pray for them because he knows we are not ready. You pray that you may be the one selected for that cherished post of power and responsibility, but God answers, "Not yet"; for God knows how frail your heart still is, he sees how many people would be hurt by errors you would lay upon them, and he loves you all too much to give you yet the treasure which you seek. Or you pray that you may have all wisdom and all knowledge, but God answers, "Not yet"; for already God must wonder whether he has let us have the knowledge of atomic energy before we had the moral stature to control it, he understands the havoc which a man can cause whose mind is greater than his soul, and he cares too much about his children to leave bread knives in their nurseries and pistols in their playrooms.

"Not yet," God sometimes answers us in prayer, "not yet. Other things have I to reveal to you, but you cannot bear them now. You are not strong enough. You are not wise enough. You are not pure enough. Not yet. Not yet."

But if God sometimes postpones the granting of our requests, he often answers them at once in ways unrecognized and unexpected. "We are always to think of God's power in terms of his purpose," Leslie Weatherhead has written. "If what he did by sheer omnipotence defeated his purpose, then, however startling and impressive, it would be an expression of weakness, not of power." For example, he says, consider a woman who has been grievously ill. She is adored by her husband to the point of foolishness, and during her convalescence he carries her from room to room, out into the garden, down to the orchard, back up the stairs to bed again; and never does he let her do a single thing to help herself. But finally the doctor intervenes. "If you do not stop denying her the means of strength," he says, "your wife will never walk again." The husband sees the point, and day after day he watches his wife walk about the house in trembling insecurity, sees her fall, and stands by as she struggles to her feet again. It would be so easy to rush to her side and carry her around once more, and to the casual observer that would seem to be an expression of power and strength. But in reality it would be the refuge of ignorance;

for it would defeat the purpose which the husband cherishes for his wife: it would keep her from walking again.

"The individual who, having prayed for patience, meets on arising from his knees the one person most irritating to him without recognizing in the incident an immediate answer to prayer, has failed to understand that patience can never be won except in the presence of that which irritates." "God may not answer prayers," it has been said, "but God always answers people." For people it is God's purpose that in the course of their earthly life they shall come to know him, have fellowship with him, love him, and share with him the works of goodness and compassion. It is his purpose that they shall have life and have it more abundantly, and when, seeking that purpose, men and women pray for things which would defeat it, God answers their souls, not their lips, and seeming to deny them, he most surely grants them their request. And so it happens that many a man has found his prayers answered not by the removal of his burden but by the doubling of his strength.

And then finally, sometimes God answers our prayers with a direct "Yes!" "There comes a moment," writes C. S. Lewis, "when children who have been playing at burglars hush suddenly: was that a *real* footstep in the hall?" And there comes a moment when people who have long been praying suddenly are startled: as surely as they strike their shins against a chair, they have struck their souls against a something in the world beyond them. They have bumped into something real, something which responds to them, something which blesses them; and just when they least expected to do so, they have suddenly found themselves in the very presence of him whom they have sought.

Sometimes the answer to their prayer is peace. Such peace as the conductor had in mind for the woman with the suitcase. Running desperately across the platform, she had just managed to catch the crowded streetcar, but when she was safely aboard, the conductor noticed that she stood in the aisle still clinging tightly to her heavy suitcase. "Lady," he said, "you can put your suitcase down now. The car will carry it for you."

Sometimes the answer to prayer is forgiveness. Such a cleansing sense of being new as I longed to find in that landlocked lake which I saw while flying down the coast of Maine one bright and sunny August morning. The water was brackish and stagnant, and look as I would, I could find neither inlet nor outlet. But the lake was on the very edge of the coast itself, and the land that kept it from the ocean could not have been more than a few short yards in width. Souls grow stale as that lake was stale, and suddenly in prayer it has been known to happen that the great seas of God break down the bar and flood the life with purity again.

And sometimes the answer to prayer is the final rock of certainty which man cannot manufacture for himself or other men destroy beneath him. It is the rock which Paul describes so well in words that fairly sing themselves to men today "Who shall separate us from the love of Christ?" he asks. "Shall tribulation, or distress, or persecution, or famine, or nakedness, or peril, or sword?" "Nay," he answers himself, "in all these things we are more than conquerors through him that loved us. For . . . neither death, nor life, nor angels, nor principalities, nor powers, nor things present, nor things to come, nor height, nor depth, nor any other creature, shall be able to separate us from the love of God, which is in Christ Jesus our Lord" (Rom. 8:35, 37-39).

God is the source of all strength and all power. God was before the worlds began; he is today; and he still will be, though the very universe itself should be destroyed. Of all the adjectives descriptive of this almighty and eternal God, the surest ones are those of love, and this love of God suffers long and is kind. It is not puffed up, and it does not seek its own. It "bears all things, believes all things, hopes all things, endures all things" (I Cor. 13:7).

All prayers are answered—sometimes by "No," sometimes by "Not yet," sometimes in ways unrecognized and unexpected. But blessed moments come when man has so attuned his soul to God that what he wishes is as God himself has willed, and then he meets God's "Yes" in that form which is the answer God reserves for those who truly pray in Jesus' name: he knows that nothing, literally nothing, can separate him from God's power, from God's eternity, from God's love, and he knows that every other man stands equally in God's concern. And in that knowledge all his other prayers are answered too; for having everything, he can ask for nothing.

9

Let every thing that hath breath
praise the Lord. Praise ye the Lord.
　　　　　—Ps. 150:6

Praise God!

LATE one afternoon my wife and I boarded the "Queen Mary" in Southampton. The great ship would lie in the docks that night and on the morrow cross the channel to Cherbourg and thence turn west for New York. Until we sat down for dinner, I had not known how hungry I was, but when the steward put the menu in my hands, suddenly I felt as if I had been starved.

The meal began with grapefruit, and from the customary courses of soup and fish, it made its way to roast chicken and then passed on to come to rest at last with steamed fedora pudding richly garnished with ice cream. To eat that night was ecstasy not often known, and yet there was agony in my heart as I ate, and I often felt like sweeping all the dishes from the table and begging God's forgiveness for the evil that I did.

The past ten weeks I had spent in Britain, ranging back

and forth across the island all the way from Plymouth on the southern coast to Scotland's Inverness, and I had daggers in me from the things that I had seen. Sugar was scarce in England. Candy was scarce, and fruits and fats and raisins. Cheese was scarce, and tea and cream and eggs. As I took another piece of chicken, it seemed as if a voice reminded me of things I wished I might forget. "Do you remember that old vicar in London?" it said. "Do you remember that faithful, gentle pastor and his wife who shared with you so willingly the little that they had? They can buy only seventeen cents worth of meat in the course of a week!" I spread another swirl of butter on my roll, and the voice was at my ear again. "Have you forgotten the poor widow in Newark? Her ration book allows her a quarter of a pound of butter a week, but she does not have the money to buy it. So she sells her butter coupon to a neighbor and uses the money for food more capable of filling empty places in the stomachs of her children."

We had made friends in Britain. Not just acquaintances. Friends. And as we took our fill that night, it was as if they stood around us at the table. They did not ask for anything. They were too proud for that. They only looked—and by their looking tore our souls apart. We wanted to thank God for the food set before us, but God seemed far away that night, and I wondered whether God wanted us to hear again those words of Joseph when his kinsmen had come down to Egypt without his beloved brother Benjamin. "Ye shall not see my face," he said, "except your brother be with you" (Gen. 3:3). And was God like Joseph? We wanted to thank God for the food set before us, but how could we find the words? "I thank thee, God, that I am not as my friends in Britain. I thank thee that I have all this fine food to eat. I thank thee that I am not hungry, that I am not rationed, that I do not have to worry any longer about getting all the meat I want, all the butter, all the eggs." That sounded strangely like a certain Pharisee who stood up one day in the temple at Jerusalem; and the words were dead before they could be spoken.

The praise of God is a Christian duty, but praise is not easy today. Thanksgiving comes hard. And if we want our worship and adoration to stand against the winds which the times blow down upon them, they must have much deeper roots than many of us give them.

There is an air of unreality in many of our formal services of thanksgiving. "Serve the Lord with gladness," the call to worship commands us. "Enter into his gates with thanksgiving, and into his courts with praise." The congregation then sings the "Gloria Patri" or perhaps the "Doxology," but have you ever watched your neighbor's face as he sang, ever watched the minister's face, ever thought about your own? The words are being sung all right, but if there is any fullness of meaning behind them, it certainly is not apparent. And the reason lies imbedded in the story of the two Arabs whom Lawrence of Arabia took with him to London. They were entranced by the gadgets of Western civilization, and as they were leaving, Lawrence asked them what they would like as a gift to take home. They said they wanted two hot-water faucets!

You cannot produce praise at the point of its audible issue any more than you produce hot water at the place of its tangible appearance. Praise is a matter of the life, not of the lips. It is the voice of the heart, not of the tongue. And if it is true that where your treasure is, there your heart is also, then where your treasure is, there, too, is your praise. What our hearts are set upon, what our lives are committed to, what we believe in, strive after, hope for—these are the substance of our true life of praise, and if the sound denies the substance, the reality is still in the substance, not in the sound. Either we praise God with all our souls, or we do not praise God. Either our thanks rise up from the deep marrow of being, or they do not rise. And if the songs of joy die soundless on the lips that tried to sing them, the chance is good that they were only ghosts of what they claimed to be, counterfeits, copies, facsimilies. Disembodied thanksgiving is heresy. The proper praise of God is always incarnate.

So the substance of praise is labor, and the essence of thanks is commitment. We do not praise God when we do not fight beside him, nor can we thank him while we disobey him. To stand for truth, not falsehood; to work for justice, not discrimination; to build, not to destroy; to help, not to hurt; to love, not to hate—these are the real songs of thanksgiving. These are the true paeans of praise.

The trouble with so many of us is that we approach God

as one mourner did a corpse. At a funeral home attendants noticed the man bend over a woman's body and fondly clasp her hand in a final gesture of affectionate farewell, and it was only later that they also noticed that the woman's ring was missing from her finger. That is our common way with God. We approach him fawningly. We come to him caressingly. But when we praise him, it is usually because he has done us a favor; and when we thank him, it is either because we have got something from him in the past or because we hope to get something from him in the future.

We too frequently forget that the Christian praise of God is not so much thanks for favors rendered as co-operation in a purpose shared, and there is a good example of that kind of praise in the little story Mrs. William Wallace wrote when she came back from the pediatrician's office. She had been considerably shocked by the sight of two children whom another woman had brought to the office. The little girl had something wrong with her legs and could not walk without crutches, and when the little boy came out of the inner office, it was obvious that one of his arms was hopelessly shriveled. "That mother has a hard row to hoe," Mrs. Wallace said to the doctor as she went into the inner office herself, and then the doctor told her what the children's story really was. "That woman is one of the happiest people I know," he said. "She had a sorry childhood—her father in a mental hospital, her mother obsessed by the fear that his illness would be transmitted to the daughter. She met her husband on a train as she was going to visit her dad. His mother was a patient there, too. Later, when they wanted to be married, they came to me. I told them what I knew—darned little—and they decided to go ahead but never to have children. However, they asked me to help them adopt a baby—'Not a picturebook one, guaranteed perfect, but one with the cards stacked against it.' " So the doctor found Pete for them, the boy with the shriveled arm; and when Pete was four, he found them Meg, the girl with the crippled legs. "And now they are going to adopt another one," the doctor said. "As soon as Meg is walking, a boy who has been battling rheumatic fever all his life is joining them. They are raising the finest family in my whole practice!" [1]

That is the way the Christian rightly praises God. He gets on the side of the good. He gets on the side of the true. He gets on the side of the brave and the fair and the right. He co-operates with God and throws himself wholeheartedly behind the one embracing purpose God reveals to him. He praises God with his life, and if he sometimes does use words to praise him, they are not hollow, empty words; they have the weight of life behind them.

But praising God means also praising people. Wrote John Masefield:

It is a rare and, when just, a noble thing to praise. Few people praise enough. All ought to praise whenever they see something that can be praised. Once in a century a man may be

[1] From *Reader's Digest*, May, 1950. Used by permission.

ruined, or for the time made insufferable by praise, but surely once in a minute something generous dies for want of it. I once heard someone say, "The occupation of heaven is praise." [2]

Praise ought also to be the occupation of earth, but it is not. When my wife cooks rice, I let her know I do not like it. But when she cooks mashed potatoes, I do not praise her; I just take her good sense for granted. When President Truman nominates an ambassador to the Vatican, I dash off a letter of vigorous protest. But when he stands firm for racial justice all over the nation, I do not praise him; I just wonder why he did not do it sooner. When members of my congregation stay in bed instead of going to church, I lament to them their lack of loyalty. But when they rise at five o'clock in the morning in Maine and drive a hundred miles to be in church on time, I do not praise them; I just look for someone else to criticize.

Praise is a demonstration of power, but we are too many times too weak to praise, too fearful, too jealous, too small. My praise can help my brother, but if I count my brother a competitor of mine, if I find in him a menace to my own security or advancement, I do not want to help my brother, and so I do not praise him. Praise is a demonstration of power, and it is only the strong who really can praise.

But praise is also a demonstration of goodness. It is evidence that a man loves righteousness and competence— even in someone else beside himself. It proves that a man is

[2] *Dead Ned*, p. 11.

mature and dependable. It shows that he stands on God's side in the struggles of earth, that he puts God's kingdom above his own, and is not guilty of the ultimate idolatry wherein a man sets himself in God's place and claims for himself the praise due only God.

We ought to seize every chance we have to praise goodness, to praise faithfulness and honesty and courage. This is a part of the praise of God. It is a part of what it means to give thanks. It is the surest witness to our own sincerity, and it puts us on the side of the angels.

And now it can be said that praising God is no more difficult today than ever in the history of men. We can sing the Lord's song in a strange land, and indeed, we must there sing it. If praising God is a thing of the life, not of the lips; if praising God is the voice of the heart, not of the tongue; if praising God means obeying God's will, standing by God's side, fighting for God's cause—then the need for praise is greater now than ever before in the lives of most of us.

One day in London I talked with a vicar whose church had been bombed in World War II. It was about eleven o'clock at night that the bomb had landed, he said, an incendiary which lodged itself in a corner of the roof beyond the reach of ladders, and by midnight the awful blaze had reached its height. "I was seventy-two years old when that happened," the vicar said, "and as I watched the fire burning down my church, I knew the end had come for me." But just as it became surely apparent that no help of man could save the great building from ruin, down from its huge stone tower came the sound of the clock striking twelve. "I am still here!" it seemed to be saying. "I, the church, am still here! And I will be here. I will always be here." "That gave me back my hope," the vicar told me. "I knew then that my church would rise again." And it did.

Praise is more important than many people think. Praise can be the difference between success and failure. It can turn the tide of defeat into triumph. It can be the straw that breaks the back of God's opposition. It can be the added ounce of energy God uses to make his will incarnate. It is a good thing to have allies when you have your enemy retreating before you, when the sun of hope is shining on your moving armies and your mighty host sweeps forward toward a certain victory; but how much more of gratitude you feel for those who come to aid you when the battle turns against you, when the night clamps down its darkness on the things you hold more dear than life and your serried ranks give ground before a ruthless foe.

Praise God today? Praise God in such a time as this? Praise God while all the things we love seem sinking into a quicksand whence we never can retrieve them? Yes! Praise God today! Praise God now more than ever! In a rural church in England I found this inscription to the man who had built it: "In the year 1653, when all things sacred were throughout ye nation either demolished or profaned, Sir Robert Shirley, Baronet, did found this church: Whose singular praise it is to have done the best things in the worst times, and hoped them in the most calamitous." "When the world is at its worst, Christians ought to be at their best." You can use your candle snuffer when the dawn breaks bright beyond the eastern hills. But when the darkness comes, you need your matches.

*If I say, Surely the darkness shall
cover me; even the night shall be
light about me.* —Ps. 139:11

10

We Journey in
the Light

ONE of the most tragic aspects of our time is the wide-
spread sense of futility. "What's the use?" we ask.
What's the use trying to be decent when other people
make no attempt to live by the same standards? What's the
use being good when good people suffer just as many
hardships as bad people? What's the use working for peace
when all the meaningful decisions are made in Washington
and nothing we do ourselves seems to matter at all? What's
the use trying to stay in college or otherwise to educate
ourselves for worthy living when the likelihood is great
that we shall soon be drafted and then permitted nothing
but the life and motives of a soldier? What's the use trying
to get ahead in our professions when wars keep infesting
the earth, and high prices and high taxes take away the

affluence and comfort we had hoped for, longed for, worked for?

Upon the tombstones of a former generation one sometimes finds the cynical inscription: "I was. I am not. I do not care." There is that attitude in many people now—that blindness of vision, that emptiness of meaning, that surrender to despondency. It is not good that this is true, and toward your own encouragement and confidence I set before you certain thoughts which have their lodgment on the solid ground of Christian faith. Five affirmations I have in mind, and I pray that God may let them be the needed rock on which some troubled soul may find his steadiness and stand.

First, then, this: When some people ask the question "What's the use?" the only honest answer you can give them is, "There isn't any!" What's the use trying to be rich? What's the use trying to be famous? What's the use trying to be successful? What's the use trying to have two cars in the garage, a winter trip to Florida, a butler and a maid? The implication is that the condition of the world has made these luxuries impossible and that life has therefore lost its meaning, and frequently these people do not understand that long before the threat of war descended on the earth again, such luxuries were just as powerless to give life meaning as they are today. There really is no use in seeking them too earnestly today, but neither was there any use in seeking them too earnestly ten years ago, fifty years ago, a hundred years ago.

For the fact is inescapable that when we make these ends the all-embracing goals of life, they are goals unworthy of the life which God has given us. Fame, prestige, wealth, comfort, power—they are not worth the price we often have to pay for them. Not worth the jealousy and envy. Not worth the sleeplessness and worry. Not worth the hardness of heart, the ruthlessness, the greed. "We cannot get grace from gadgets," J. B. Priestly has written. "The dishes in the bakelite houses of the future may not break, but the heart can. A man may be as unhappy in the spun glass trousers of tomorrow as he is today in worsted ones. Even a man with six bathrooms may find life flat, stale, and unprofitable."

The frame of mind which man has always needed is the one which Paul described in writing to the Philippians. "I have learned," he told them, "in whatsoever state I am, therewith to be content. I know both how to be abased, and I know how to abound: everywhere and in all things I am instructed both to be full and to be hungry, both to abound and to suffer need" (Phil. 4:11-12). In the goals which many people have set for their lives there is nothing essentially wrong, but neither is there anything especially significant, and when they think that the loss of them has taken away their life's meaning, they prove only that their life never had much of any meaning anyway. There is no use in setting our hearts too anxiously upon such ends as these, and the reason is not that so much of our money is being siphoned off into high prices and high taxes. The reason is simply that the true significance of human life cannot be found in them.

But not all doubts about the meaning of our lives are born of such misguided understanding, and the second of the affirmations deals with some of them which have a little better parentage. Here it is: Human personality is more important than anything else in God's world. One day the gatekeeper at a famous race track drew his life's savings out of the bank and sent the entire $1,200 to his nephew to help him through college. When asked why he did it, he had a simple explanation. "Day in and day out," he said, "I watch men bet on horses and lose their shirts. The way I figure it, a fellow might stand a chance to make a killing if he bets on a human being." And that attitude is basic in the Christian faith.

People stand at the top of God's creation. The world exists for man, not man for the world, and although man can bring destruction to the world without the world's consent, the world cannot destroy man without man's own permission. For although men and women have affinities with the earth and the things of the earth, their real homeland is in the realm of the soul; and the soul cannot be reached by any weapon in the arsenals of earth. You cannot shoot the soul. You cannot stab it or burn it or tear it to shreds. God so loved people that he sent his only-begotten Son to give his life for them, and people are priceless. God so loved people that he made their souls invulnerable to earthly harm, and people have no need for fear.

It is therefore not of major moment that good people suffer just as many hardships as bad people. It is the soul that counts, and hardships cannot reach the soul. It is loving God that matters, and hardships cannot keep us from that love. It is serving God that gives our lives their meaning, and hardships cannot hold us from that service. Pain, disappointment, frustration, injustice—these are unfortunate but not decisive. Without our permission they can trouble the surface of our lives, but not the depths. Without our consent they can ruffle the fringes of our beings, but not the real fabric itself.

Nor need it be an utter tragedy that military service keeps us for a while from things we really want to do. No man walks alone who walks with God, and he who stood above the cross at Calvary will surely go with those who bear their burdens over rocky ways today. The man who really loves God will never be helpless to serve him. He may be denied the choice of weapons, but no one can keep him from using to the best advantage those he has. He may be forced to work in unwanted surroundings, but no one can prevent him from obeying God's will within the limits of the circumstances which have been imposed upon him.

It is the purpose of earthly life that we grow in understanding, in love, and in readiness to serve the highest good which we can find. Those are the proper goals of human beings, and there is always use in striving for them; for however grievously life treats us, however far war carries us, however sorely other people injure us, those goals cannot be pulled beyond our grasp. They are always present. They are always possible.

The third affirmation is this: Suffering can be used to do for us what unbroken happiness can never do. Wrote Leslie Weatherhead:

> This man has good luck, and that man has bad luck, but *I wonder whether, in the sight of God, there is any real difference between good luck and bad luck.* . . . Dives thought he had good luck and Lazarus bad, but in the next world things looked very different, and—if we *must* use time words—we shall be longer there than here. . . . Life cannot ultimately be unjust. I have seen the lucky ones finish their lives having made a very poor thing of their luck, and I have seen the unlucky ones turn the rough stones of ill luck over and find they were jewels, and turn the things we call calamities into a pattern of loveliness and a pathway for other feet. . . . "All things work together for good to them that love God." [1]

Well-favored people often have to bear burdens which less favored people neither know nor recognize. Jesus said, "It is easier for a camel to go through the eye of a needle, than for a rich man to enter into the kingdom of God" (Matt. 19:24). "Tropic seas do not breed many geniuses," someone has written. "The devil likes to summer in cool places," another man has said. And in the sufferings and deprivations with which the average man or woman is confronted, there is no greater obstacle to successful living than that faced by many people who appear to face no obstacles at all.

[1] *When the Lamp Flickers*, p. 62.

Indeed, it may be even that in their very hardships these seemingly less favored people have the finest building stones for lasting life which any man could ever have. There has been a great deal of cynicism about the ancient dictum that "whom the Lord loveth he chasteneth" (Heb. 12:6), but many are the men who have found that sometimes God actually works in that way. "Ye thought evil against me," Joseph once said to his brothers while talking to them of their treachery to him, "but God meant it unto good" (Gen. 50:20). I suppose that Joseph was simply exercising what Alfred Adler calls "the human being's power to turn a minus into a plus." I suppose that he was doing only what the psalmist had in mind in speaking of the people who "passing through the valley of Weeping . . . make it a place of springs" (Ps. 84:6 A.S.V.). I suppose that he had found that truth which Robert Browning Hamilton discovered many centuries later and put in his poem "Along the Road":

> I walked a mile with Pleasure.
>   She chattered all the way,
> But left me none the wiser
>   For all she had to say.
>
> I walked a mile with Sorrow,
>   And ne'er a word said she;
> But, oh, the things I learned from her
>   When Sorrow walked with me!

Sorrow need not squeeze the meaning out of life. It can, in fact, give life a wholly new significance. There is use in facing sorrow with good cheer and with courage; for through the strength that sorrow gives, a mighty host of men have come to say as one man said, "It is good for me that I have been afflicted" (Ps. 119:71).

And then the fourth affirmation: In this day and in this place no Christian has the right to turn back from the fighting line and slink away as if the great crusade of Christian hope had been already lost. On the level of the nations we often hear it said today that there is nothing which the individual citizen can do to swing the coming days away from war toward peace. That is nonsense! To be sure, the whole weight of public thinking is often in the opposite direction. To be sure also, it is frequently assumed that any talk of peace is little short of treachery. But this is still a democratic country. Our representatives are still elected representatives. In terms of the present moment most of them will respond rather quickly to the expressed will of large numbers of their constituents, and in terms of the future they can be ousted if they do not respond. Political parties are made up of people, and Christian people have as much chance as anybody else to take control of them. Political offices are occupied by people, and followers of Christ have just as great an opportunity as anyone else to be elected to them. We can have international peace if we want it, and the reason we do not have it is not that peace is impossible but simply that we have not wanted it badly enough.

Nor is it otherwise on the level of the individual himself. "What's the use trying to be decent," we ask, "when so many other people take the shorter way and seem to prosper?" In one sense that question is like asking why we should be content with meat, vegetables and milk while other people can have whisky and narcotics. Decency is its own reward and needs no props from earthly circumstance or worldly pleasure. But even more important is the fact that the degree in which the evil of the world removes life's meaning from us is almost in direct proportion to the carelessness with which we take Jesus' counsel that "it is more blessed to give than to receive" (Acts 20:35). If our lives are organized in accordance with the reverse of that counsel, then the presence of evil can well bring us down to despair. But if we take Jesus seriously, if we really believe in the deeps of our being that it is a more godlike state to be on the giving end of things than to be on the getting end of things, then the present state of the world becomes a matter of no decisive moment, and it could even be said that the worse the state of the world, the deeper life's possible meaning.

We have lost many battles, we Christians, but we have not lost the war. There is use in fighting for the good we love, because that good has still the chance for victory. And when other people are at their weakest, the need for us is at its strongest.

But of all the reasons for confidence and courage, the fifth affirmation brings to mind the greatest: "God is not mocked" (Gal. 6:7). Too many people try to put themselves in God's place. Too many people try to hold the world up with their own hands. Too many people forget that human beings are not alone in the world, that God is still in control of his own universe, and that when men have done their worst and best, those words from the opening of the Lambeth Conference of 1930 still speak a needed truth:

> While we deliberate, He reigns;
> When we decide wisely, He reigns;
> When we decide foolishly, He reigns;
> When we serve Him humbly, loyally, He reigns;
> When we serve Him self-assertively, He reigns;
> When we rebel and seek to withhold our service, He reigns!

That was the confidence which lay behind the closing days of Jesus' life on earth. "Behold, we go up to Jerusalem," he told his disciples, "and the Son of man shall be betrayed unto the chief priests and unto the scribes, and they shall condemn him to death, and shall deliver him to the Gentiles to mock, and to scourge, and to crucify him." Thus far those words of his add up to nothing but despair. "What's the use?" he might have asked. "What's the purpose? What's the meaning?" But then see how he brings that speech of his to its sudden ending: "And the third day he shall rise again" (Matt. 20:18-19). It is only there you have the victory. It is only there you have the use, the purpose, the meaning. When Jesus rode up to the Holy

City, "a very great multitude spread their garments in the way." They "cut down branches from the trees and strewed them in the way." And those that went before and followed behind shouted out their triumph, saying, "Hosanna to the Son of David: Blessed is he that cometh in the name of the Lord; Hosanna in the highest" (Matt. 21:8-9). And what was it that gave those paeans their everlasting meaning? It was the Resurrection! It was the understanding that the Cross was not the end, that God was not mocked, that righteousness had a cosmic guarantee.

Some sorrows there are which man cannot assuage. Some problems there are which man cannot solve. Some burdens there are which man cannot carry. "What's the use?" he asks himself. But suddenly he finds an unexpected comrade at his elbow. The King himself has buckled on his armor, fastened down his helmet, taken up his shield, and thrown his matchless weight into the fighting line beside him. "In the world ye shall have tribulation," the King tells him, "but be of good cheer; I have overcome the world. . . . And I, if I be lifted up, . . . will draw all men unto me" (John 16:33; 12:32.) And in the twinkling of an eye all of the aspects of the world have been changed for that man. For he feels the great, long battle line move forward as the King moves forward. He sees the enemy fall back before them. And from the clouds above his head the sun breaks through to shed upon the earth the promise of a new day dawning for mankind. He finds that now he "journeys in the light." He knows that his life has purpose. He understands that his life can win its proper victory. And so through all the tumult round about him, he lifts his voice as men once did of old. "Hosanna to the Son of David," he cries. "Blessed is he that cometh in the name of the Lord; Hosanna in the highest."

So God created man in his own image.
                    —Gen. 1:27   **11**

You Are the
Child of a King

THE *Saturday Evening Post* once ran an article entitled
"The Big Ancestor Hunt." It said that more Americans are rushing headlong into the past than ever before in history. Five hundred persons a week pad silently
through the marble halls of the Library of Congress to the
genealogical department. In Pennsylvania they search for
old wills in ancient courthouse records. In New Jersey
they band together as "The Tombstone Hounds," seeking
clues to family trees in abandoned cemeteries. In Massachusetts people are said to value the pedigree more than
the family silver, and from Los Angeles to Long Island the
ancestor hunters are busily at work trying to find out
whence they came. "It's a long, hard job discovering
where you came from," one woman said. "It takes a lot out

of you. But you end up with pride, and it's always a comfort to know you're well descended."

It is an interesting phenomenon, this search for our ancestors. It is interesting because it has so many cosmic connotations. Its quest is for the ones from whom we came. It wants to know the soil in which our human plants are rooted. "Whence did I come?" it asks. "To what do I belong? Who is it that I really am?"

To that question many different answers have been given through the years. You are an animal, some men have said. All talk of spirit and soul is vain and futile dreaming. You are a cousin of the apes. You sprang with them from common prehistoric ancestors, and stripped of all your proud and pretty finery, you are essentially a beast among the other beasts.

You are a professor, other men have said. Or you are a carpenter, a storekeeper, a secretary, a housewife. That is identity enough for anyone. You are what you do, and if you want a label for yourself, then call yourself by your profession. You are a taxi driver. You are a policeman. You are a salesman.

You are Henry Smith, still other men have said. You are Alice Johnson. You are Robert Jones. Do not try to complicate the issue. Your last name is your family name, and your first is the name with which your father and your mother blessed you or afflicted you. Do not ask anybody who you are. You know yourself! You are Susan Rogers. You are Richard Hensley. You are Barbara O'Brien.

Here's a Faith for You

So the answers come. But to the man who suddenly has sensed his loneliness within the universe they do not really answer. I know I have a kinship with the animals, but in my mind and heart there is a something dog and ape will never know. My profession is a thing of choice, not of nature, and my name is but an accident of birth and preference. And so it goes with all the common answers to the question of the one I truly am. They look solid until I try to lean my faith upon them, but then they fall in ruins at my feet.

I therefore turn with all the greater eagerness to find the Christian answer to my problem, and the years since Christ proclaim to me a word disarming in its simpleness, but yet so firmly lodged within the universe that when I take my stand upon its promises, I am not and I cannot be moved. You, it says, are a child of God. On a day too old for human knowing God conceived his plan for man. Through the aeons and the centuries since then, he has so used the process which we call evolution that the creature he designed at last came forth. Year by year and one by one he works through the love of a man and a woman to bring forth from the womb of the world new life, and so you came to be yourself. Your origin is thus in him from whom came all that is or evermore shall be. You are his creature and his child. He made your being possible because he loved you and hungered that you be a something more than just a dream within his mind. He made you in his image, and he crowned you with glory and honor. You are the child of a king, and of such a king as never

118

shall be rivaled, since in all the universe there is no God save him alone.

God made you clean and pure and spotless, but he also made you free, as he himself is free, and in that freedom you have often sinned. You have erred and strayed from his ways like a lost sheep. You have done those things which you ought not to have done, and you have left undone those things which you ought to have done. You have been ignorant when you had the power to be wise. You have resolved and then broken your resolutions. And day by day your heart has harbored greed and hatred, which have twisted you and warped you into ineffectiveness.

But still the imprint of your Father's hand is fixed upon your heart. You have wandered, but you remember the homeland. You have fallen, but you have the capacity to rise again. There is something more to you than meets the eye. You are not "contained between your hat and your boots." You are a creature of God's will. You are the child of a king.

Such, in part, is what the Christian centuries have said in answer to the question "Who am I?" And in the word they give we find the power and the peace to live in such a world as we confront today, and call it good.

I still remember as a precious and cherished experience the coming of Nels Ferré to Andover Newton. He had gone to Harvard for graduate study in preparation for the ministry, and to support himself and his family during those years, he had assumed responsibility for a sizable church in one of our eastern cities. From the moment of his arrival at Harvard he made a mark for himself, and his professors soon saw that his was to be one of the truly great minds of his day.

But it was a high price that he paid. Every morning he was up at five oclock and at work in his study. The hours from eight until twelve he spent at the college. In the afternoon he was back at work among the people of the church, and in the evening he was with his books again, seldom retiring before midnight and often not until much later. The examinations for his doctorate he passed with high honors, and not even the critical professors at Harvard could find anything wrong with his dissertation.

And then the blow fell—a swift, paralyzing, crippling malady for which the doctors could make no sure diagnosis. They said that he would never walk again, but as I came to know him, I was sure that they were wrong. He had been appointed to teach at Andover Newton, and day after day I went down the Hill to get him in my car. Then at his request I began to leave the car one house, two houses, three houses from his own residence, and he would drag himself to it and fall upon the seat exhausted. Gradually we lengthened the distance—one block, two blocks, halfway up the Hill, three-quarters of the way up the Hill. I think I shall never forget that memorable day when he told me not to bring the car at all, and as he struggled up the last few feet to the summit, he burst into such a triumphant rendition of Luther's great hymn as must have startled inhabitants for miles around:

> A mighty fortress is our God,
>   A bulwark never failing;
> Our helper he, amid the flood
>   Of mortal ills prevailing.

Who am I? I am a child of God. God made me. God keeps me. And nothing life can do can separate me from his love or from his will and might to lift me up and bear me on. When illness strikes my frame, I will not forget that deeper dignity of man which no microbe ever made can touch or harm. I will remember that though this earthly tabernacle is dissolved, my untented spirit has another house, "not made with hands, eternal in the heavens" (II Cor. 5:1). I will keep in sight my calling under God, and through the mysteries of pain and disability I will so conduct myself that all my life may be a witness to the One who made me.

Should an operation face me, I will keep my fears to barest minimum, and I will not permit the hospital routines to rob me of the consciousness of whence I came, who I am, and whither I at last shall go. The trusting of myself to strange hands shall not bring terror to my soul, nor the removal of my accustomed clothing, nor the separation from my loved ones, nor the sight of the operating table, nor the thought of the surgeon's knife.

And should some sudden damming of my body's processes bring death much closer than I want, then "though I walk through the valley of the shadow of death, I will fear no evil" (Ps. 23:4), for One is with me, in whose keeping I shall yet live on. A few years ago Peter Marshall, chaplain of the United States Senate, died. "Are you scared of death?" he once had asked a congregation. "I'm not. I'm looking forward to it. I can hardly wait." I know that one day I must die, and if the need should come tomorrow that I go, I go in peace for I am not a creature of this world alone.

One day a group of Christians called upon Emperor Hirohito of Japan. They were later asked about their impressions of the man, and all of them were good. "He is modest and well educated," they said. "He is the kind of person whom we would like to know much better." "I wish," said one of them, "that some morning that man would wake up and say, 'I am king; so today I am going to do a little real kinging.'" Poverty, unemployment, bereavement, slander—I shall not permit the evils life may bring to take away my birthright. I am the child of a king. I have royal blood in my veins, and hour by hour and day by day I shall live as one who knows the man he truly is.

But in the knowledge of my origin in God I shall not be guilty of the sin of parasites. I shall take, because I have no choice. All that is belongs to God and comes from God, and it blesses me by reason of his gift of it to me. I create nothing and can create nothing. And so I take.

You Are the Child of a King

But I shall also give. Because I am God's child, I am expected to bear upon myself the likeness of my Father. I have a charge to keep. I have a vocation. I have a calling. There is a purpose for my life within God's plan, and I shall not permit that purpose to be thwarted by choosing my vocation with a view to nothing but personal advancement, probable income, manner of living, or choice of location. In thinking of the ends to which my life is given, I shall substitute "concern" for "profit," and though my work is making me rich, I shall leave that work if it does not make a contribution for the higher life of man upon the earth. I shall get rid of the notion that church work is necessarily more Christian than other kinds of work, and I shall make myself remember that any worthy toil can be just as much a calling under God as the ministry or priesthood. I shall ponder often thoughts like those of him who said that if the purpose of God in the creation of the world is to go on, then children must be born and nurtured in body and mind; and that calls for the vocation of fathers and mothers. And since life cannot go on without food and clothing and houses, all who share in the production and distribution of the common necessities of life serve the purpose of God. And since the life of man as God wills it would be much poorer if it were limited to the bare necessities, God is served, too, by all those who create beauty, those who think and teach, even those whose talent is for comedy and laughter. All these "are truly called in their work to the service of God's purpose for his world and for man." All these are working in areas which are "tragically distorted and turned from their true end by our self-centeredness and self-assertiveness." And all these are asked of God to make their daily work a thing of holiness by reason of its setting in his purposes.

One day in Ireland Dwight L. Moody heard Henry Varley say very quietly to a group of Christian workers that "the world has yet to see what God can do with and for and through and in a man who is fully and wholly consecrated to him." Two days later Moody was in London listening to Charles Spurgeon, the great English preacher. As he sat high in the balcony, it seemed that heaven had descended on his soul; and he recalled again the words of Varley. "He said a man," thought Moody. "He did not say a great man, or a learned man, or a rich man, or a wise man, or an eloquent man, or a smart man, but simply a man. I am a man, and it lies within the man himself whether he will or will not make that entire and full consecration. I will try my utmost to be that man."

Who am I? I am a messenger. I am a herald. I am an ambassador. I was put upon the earth for a purpose. I have a mission to fulfill, a goal to achieve, a task to perform; and life is too short for me to tarry over things that slow my feet upon the road. So what strength I have, I give to him who made me, and pray that I may so be guided day by day, that in the end my life may serve a useful purpose in God's kingdom. For God has made me but "a little lower than the angels" (Ps. 8:5), and "unto whom-

soever much is given, of him shall be much required"
(Luke 12:48).

So I am not alone in the universe, and my success or failure
does not depend upon the turn of chance or the will of
man. I came from God. I dwell in God. I go to God. I
am his creature, and I am his child. I ought therefore to
act as if I were. I ought to be at peace within myself, and
I ought to give my life to more than selfish purposes.

So shall it henceforth be. For God is my refuge and my
strength. Therefore I shall not fear, "though the earth be
removed, and though the mountains be carried into the
midst of the sea" (Ps. 46:2).

The Mighty Are
the Meek

THE words of Jesus often seem to be conflicting words. "Do not blow your own horn," he tells his disciples. "Be meek. Be lowly in heart. Be poor in spirit. Be humble." But it is the same man speaking to the same people who gives that other counsel too, "Let your light so shine before men, that they may see your good works."

There is apparent contradiction in those two commandments, and to the confusion thus engendered there must be added the fact that we do not really want to obey either of them. We are too selfish to be easily humble and too Christian to be openly proud, and so we stand with one foot lodged in either wagon track and wishing mightily that we could pull ourselves together.

Yet both commandments are legitimate commandments.

126

Both occupy a place tremendously important in our Christian faith and practice. And to that Christian faith and practice both bear the same relationship as air and water to our earthly life: we simply cannot get along with only one of them.

What then does it mean to be humble? And how can our humility be reconciled with the need to let our light so shine before men, as Jesus said, that they may see our good works?

For one thing, if being humble inescapably involves the wisdom not to overestimate ourselves, it just as inescapably involves the courage not to underestimate ourselves. We are not to be puffed up, but neither are we to be deflated. We are not to vaunt ourselves, but neither are we to despise ourselves.

Rufus Jones once told a little tale about the daughter of a prosperous farmer who came into a village store in Maine. Wanting to be friendly, the storekeeper smiled and started talking with her. "Are your hens laying now?" he asked. "They can," the girl replied with her nose in the air, "but of course in our financial position they don't have to." Unwarranted pride is quickly recognized in everyone except ourselves, and even in ourselves we are sufficiently aware of it to need no lengthy proof that it is incompatible with true humility in Christian men and women.

But it is just as incompatible with true humility that we undervalue ourselves as that we overvalue ourselves. It has been said that "pride in our own humility is one of the devil's own tricks," and many a Uriah Heep is really not a humble man at all but in the deepest sense a vain man, an arrogant man, a pretentious man. People are the handiwork of God. They are the creatures of his will and his labor. He made them to be but "a little lower than the angels," and granted them dominion over all the world in which they live (Ps. 8:5-6). The least of us is precious past all price, and all the diamonds in all the world are nothing but a bin of broken glass when you try to buy with them a single human life. You have that stature under God, and I have it, and to waste ourselves is not a sign of humility but an evidence of ignorance or sin. To despise yourself is to hurl an insult in God's face. It is effrontery, insolence, arrogance.

Among other things, being humble means knowing why God put you here. It means taking an inventory of yourself and seeing yourself without distortion. It means neither overestimating yourself nor underestimating yourself.

In the second place, the most successful Christians are not always the most "successful." "Whosoever exalteth himself shall be abased," Jesus said, "and he that humbleth himself shall be exalted" (Luke 14:11). We know enough about human life, however, to be convinced that it does not always work out that way. In the hurly-burly of modern business the man who humbles himself is not half so likely to be exalted as to be kicked in the pants, and there are few of us in any walk of life who have never noticed instances where being humble seemed synonymous with being a failure.

This troubles us more than it should; for it is history's record that many of the world's most accomplished Christians have appeared to their contemporaries to be among their day's most unsuccessful people. Jesus was regarded as a traitor by the state and the synagogue. Stephen was stoned and Peter crucified. Paul was a person wholly unacceptable in almost every town to which he went. Francis of Assisi was a beggar. John Wycliffe was expelled from Oxford. John Bunyan and Isaac Watts were jailed.

This country is sufficiently a Christian country to encourage the illusion that being "successful" and being a successful Christian are always compatible, and even that one of Christianity's most important purposes is to beget this coveted prosperity in those who keep the faith without fail. But we frequently forget that a man is not rightly first a doctor and then a Christian, or first an insurance salesman and then a Christian, or first a lawyer and then a Christian. He is rightly first a Christian and only secondly a member of his calling or profession. The Christian's primary vocation is that of being a Christian. It is to know the God revealed in Jesus Christ; and because God's thoughts are not always our thoughts nor his ways our ways, being successful in the eyes of the world need not always mean being successful in God's eyes, nor will failing in the world's way always mean that we have failed in God's way.

Being humble involves the willingness to be reckoned a

failure in everyone's sight but God's. It involves substituting for man's standard of values God's standard of values. It involves renunciation, denial, sacrifice.

But, third, this should come as no surprise to any one of us, because as Christians we have freely chosen to be placed in a special category wholly separate from ordinary men.

When a soldier goes into battle, he knows that he will doubtless have to bear great hardship, deprivation, and pain. He understands that other men will be trying to hurt him, and that he faces the possibility of being wounded or even killed. To the intelligent soldier none of these facts are matters for astonishment. When he enlisted or when he was drafted, he knew that these possibilities were an inescapable part of military service, and sooner or later he learns to take them in his stride and not to be embittered by them.

So it rightly is with being a Christian. We have lifted our heads above the crowd, and the likelihood is great that somebody will throw something at us. We have volunteered to bear a cross, and the chance is good that life will take us up on it. We have said that we do not want to become masters but servants, and we can scarcely blame the ones who take us at our word. No man should choose garbage collecting as his lifework unless he is willing to empty garbage pails. No woman should aspire to be a schoolteacher unless she is ready to work with children. And no more should a man be a Christian unless he is prepared to bear the load the Christian life demands.

For, from the Christian point of view, being humble

means seeking God's kingdom first. It means putting God's will above your own. And because God's will is so different from man's will, it means bearing a very heavy burden. For sacrifice is as inseparable from true humility as water is from swimming.

Yet, in the fourth place, it should be said at once that any sacrifice demanded by the Christian faith should never be regarded as an end in itself, but always as a means. When the Christian is asked to lay down his life, to discount his own importance, to carry a cross, to turn the other cheek, to go the second mile, to be humble—it is always for a purpose. There is nothing to be gained by tormenting one-self simply for the sake of being tormented, denying desires simply for the sake of seeing those desires denied, being crushed simply for the sake of being crushed. Christians are counseled to have the harmlessness of doves, but they are also counseled to have the wisdom of serpents (Matt. 10:16); and there is no wisdom in letting yourself be defeated or destroyed unless some high and holy purpose will be served by your defeat or destruction. Christianity is frequently regarded as irrational, but unless it represents the highest reason, then it ought to be repudiated altogether. We believe that God created us out of much labor and striving. We believe that he loves us and has a purpose for us in the world. We cannot therefore cast upon the rubbish heap these lives which God has dearly bought, and the only reason for the sacrifice of self is that higher ends than selfish ends will be served by that sacrifice.

That is the only thing which saves Christ's crucifixion from the category of despair and degradation. Jesus died for a purpose. His crucifixion was part of a plan, and out of the very evil of men his agony became the instrument whereby love could work its will upon the world. For Christian thought and life Calvary has never been an end in itself: it has always been the means by which we reach the empty tomb in Joseph's garden.

And so it is today. For being humble does not mean unhitching the horse from your wagon and sitting in the road until someone smashes into you and kills you. It means hitching your wagon to a star, being lifted up to points of lofty vision, seeing purposes that have no end in time or space, surrendering yourself to those purposes, and finding in the sacrifice which they demand the seal of greater victory than you otherwise could have even dreamed of.

Thus it is that finally we come to see how humility is fully consonant with letting your light so shine before men that they may see your good works, how such a display is not a sign of arrogance at all but a witness to the deepest possible modesty. You have made commitment of your life to something more important than yourself—more important than what other people think about you, say about you, do about you. Your light is not your own light, and it pertains to you only in the sense that you happen to be the channel through which it reaches out to other people. It is not your creation any more than the electricity which flows through a wire is the creation of the wire, and when you let your light shine before men, it is not that men may see your glory, but that they may see God's glory.

You will find a great deal in Jesus' words about the hypocrisy of praying in public places, doing alms before men, letting other people see you fast, coveting the chief seats in the synagogues. But times have changed since Jesus' day, and the real hypocrites in most churches are not the people who profess more faith than they have, but those who have more faith than they profess. Most churches today do not have much trouble with men and women who talk too much about their Christian faith, but they have a great deal of trouble with people who act as if they were ashamed of their Christian faith. And with most of those people the difficulty is not that they are too humble but that they are too proud—too proud to admit their indebtedness to God and to Christ, too proud to risk ridicule or rebuff, too proud to undergo the discipline of trial and failure, too proud to dedicate their lives to something greater than their lives. Among most Christians there is not much danger from the public vaunting of our faith and practice. Many of us would rather be found dead than found praying. If we give money to a worthy cause, we want it kept secret lest some other worthy cause approach us for a like donation. We enjoy food too much to fast, and far from struggling for the front seats in the church, we come early so that we can sit in the back and be less conspicuous.

But Christians ought never to forget that they are a chosen people—chosen not for privilege but for responsibility. We have a job to do, and humility does not consist in being too proud to bear its burden, but in being sufficiently aware of the job's importance to give the job precedence over any hope or fear we have ourselves. The psalmist wrote of old, "Let the redeemed of the Lord say so" (Ps. 107:2). "I wish it were possible," said Dick Sheppard, "to persuade men and women how much the cause of Christ needs their spoken witness. Perhaps there is nothing England so needs today as that those who set store by Christianity and wish it well should say so." Jesus was speaking to his own disciples when he uttered those words in the Sermon on the Mount. "Ye are the light of the world," he had been telling them, and then he speaks those probing, prodding, goading words that strike the heart of every one of us, "If therefore the light that is in thee be darkness, how great is that darkness!" (Matt. 6:23.) In such a time as this where will you go for light if not to the Christian faith, and where will you find the Christian faith except in Christian people?

Under such circumstances we are not being humble when we hide that light under a bushel. We are only being greedy. We are only being lazy. Being humble involves the readiness to be used for gallant purposes and to be spent for noble ends. It means letting your light so shine before men that your good works may be seen to God's glory.

Thus to be humble is to be exalted, and otherwise to be exalted is to be abased. For the humble man is God's man, and the strength in which he stands is not so much his own as God's; but he who is self-exalted is no one's man but his own. He has nothing behind him but himself—nothing in him, nothing under him, nothing over him. He is not so much sinful as pathetic; and standing side by side with him who lives in power not his own, he proves with him the truth of Jesus' statement, "Whosoever exalteth himself shall be abased; and he that humbleth himself shall be exalted" (Luke 14:11).

Your Home Is a Cell

EVERY home is a cell. It is a cell in the penological sense, or it is a cell in the biological sense. It is a prison, or it is a unit of growth. It is a jail, or it is a living body. A prison is a place where people are denied their freedom, and a jail an instrument of cramping and hurting. But when you speak of cells as plants and animals and human beings have them, then all the mystery of life is bound up in them. Cells like that have vigor and vitality. They have movement and development. They have freedom and hope.

More homes are jails than many people know. More homes are dungeons, prison houses, torture chambers of the heart and soul; and of the homes which really qualify as living units in the human fellowship which God intended, the number is far smaller than we frequently suppose. For it is much simpler to turn the key in the door of a jail than to be yourself a part of decision and struggle and growth.

Your Home Is a Cell

Homes are prisons when some of their members—or all of their members—are confined by the home, immured by the home, chained by the home, entombed by the home. Such homes are found in forms beyond counting, and almost everyone has seen a sample of them somewhere.

There are homes which are jails because of the arrogance of one of their members. It may be that the father is the lord of the manor. He is the captain of the company. He is the boss. Orders are orders, and his whim is the law. He earns the money, and he determines how the money shall be spent. He provides the house, and he ordains the way in which it shall be kept. What the children should do, he tells them; how his wife should dress, he informs her. No decisions are valid without his approval, and no movement is safe without his consent. And that home is not a unit of growth but a place of confinement.

There are homes which are jails because of the illness of one of their members. Not just because the mother is sick. Not even because she is crippled or deformed or doomed to die of some incurable disease. Some of the happiest homes I know are homes where such a tragedy is found, and illness of itself cannot slam shut the prison door. That only happens when self-pity comes into the picture. Mother is not only sick but also glad that she is sick. It gets her attention. It compels the other members of the family to put her first in all their thinking. It gives her a club to hold over their heads, a chain to fasten around their ankles, a lever to pry out of them any concession she sets her heart upon. The weakest member of the family thus becomes the strongest, and that home is a jail.

And then there are homes which are jails because of greed. The values of the father and the mother have become perverted. They exalt things above people. They bow down before the god "Success." They worship at the "Altar of Gadgets." Their religion is having all the comforts of civilized living. Their cross is money, and their Bible is what the better people think. No one in the home is free to say what he wants to say, do what he wants to do, be what he wants to be. Every word and every deed must be another brick in the building of the family's affluence, the family's security, the family's social position. There is not much time for kindness. There is not much time for fun. There is not much time for peace of mind. Brick by brick the all-important walls must be constructed, and many families find out too late that what they built was not a mansion but a dungeon.

And then there are homes which are jails because of "love." It may be the "love" which a widowed mother feels for her only daughter. It would break her heart to see her daughter leave home, she tells her. She could not bear to have her get married and set up housekeeping on her own. She loves her little girl and wants her always by her side. Or it may be the "love" which parents feel for their only son. "Please don't strike Willy," a mother once wrote to Willy's teacher on the first day of school. "We never strike him at home except in self-defense." Because he is so

Your Home Is a Cell

precious to his father and his mother, Willy must never be hurt. He may not use a hammer because he might injure his finger. He may not go swimming because he might catch a cold. He may not play baseball because the ball might hit him and hurt him. Or still further, it may be the "love" a father bears his son when he approaches the choice of his vocation. He wants his son to be a lawyer, as he is himself a lawyer and his father was before him. He loves his boy, and he cannot understand how he could even dream of wanting to work with his hands. Garages are necessary, of course, but he thinks too much of his son's future ever to consent to his being a mechanic. He would be ashamed to think of him in such an occupation. Yes, sir! He would be ashamed of him! You seldom think of love as a means of confinement, but put quotation marks around it, and you will find that prison bars are often made of it.

The lust which sometimes leads a man to forget that his wife is first of all a soul and only secondly a body, first of all a person and only then a female; the ignorance which often lets parents starve their children's souls as they would never think of starving their bodies; the busyness which leaves no time for comradeship and led the little boy to ask his mother, "Who is that man who comes home on Saturday nights, spanks me, and puts me to bed?" These things rob homes of freedom, take away their light and life, stunt their growth and their development, and make them nothing but stockades where prisoners are kept.

Every home is a cell, and some homes are cells in the

penological sense. They are jails. They are prisons. They are dungeons.

But some homes are cells in the biological sense, and so all homes should be. For the most part, we have no difficulty recognizing such a home when we find it. Such a home is happy. Such a home is contented. Such a home is alive and awake and alert. No member of the family feels cramped by the home, crippled by the home, thwarted by the home. The home is not a dam but a channel, and through his membership in the home each person finds not less freedom but more freedom. Everyone feels secure, and therefore no one needs to strengthen his own self-confidence by the disparagement of somebody else in the home, or by unwholesome dependence on somebody else, or by a vain display of earthly possessions and position. All the people in the home have found out who they really are and why God put them here. They are at peace with themselves, at peace with one another, at peace with God; and being thus released from the bondage of their own discontent and fear, they find themselves free—free to mature, free to prosper, free to live.

While we can generally recognize such a home when we find it, the trouble most of us face is that of building such a home in the first place. There is a multitude of ways in which the problem may be attacked, but I suggest the three which I believe are central in the building of a home as God intended homes to be.

The first is simply the organization of the time-tested

family council. Once each week the members of the family sit down to think about the family's concerns. They sit down as equals, and though the father's vote and mother's vote may carry greater weight than the small child's vote, the small child still has a vote, and his vote will not be disregarded. Allowances, chores, vacations, the use of the car and radio and bathroom, the color of the new wallpaper, the state of the family finances, the time when daughter has to be home from the dance—all may freely be brought up for discussion. Nobody is boss. Nobody is a second-class citizen. And time and thought enough are taken so that when at last a decision is made, it is the family's decision, one in which each member of the family can vigorously concur because he helped to make it in the first place. It has been said that "families are living cells of emerging democracy." Democracy is immeasurably slower than dictatorship, but it is also immensely better. A family council takes time, but it is worth the time it takes. For it rips off the bars from the windows of the home. It unlocks the cell door. It sets the prisoners free.

In the second place, the family needs to do things together. The only reason for astonishment that so many families disintegrate is that the families themselves are astonished at their disintegration. The home is somewhat like the human body: you have to keep its parts together or you cannot keep the whole alive. And in far too many homes the procedures have been like those of a man who took a human being, chopped off his head, pulled off his arms and legs, ran a dagger through his heart, and then wondered why the human being did not function properly. At seven o'clock in the morning each member of the family pulls himself reluctantly from bed and vouchsafes a sepulchral grunt to other members of the family he passes on his way to the bathroom. Breakfast is eaten in haste or abstraction, and the family disperses for the day. At three o'clock in the afternoon the children dash in long enough to change their clothes, and at six the parents and children dutifully gather at the dinner table for a meal marked chiefly by the weariness of the parents and the eagerness of the children to hurry away to the television set or to the baseball game. By half-past eight the children are home again and by quarter of nine in bed. Then the father dozes on the divan and the mother slips away to sleep in her chair, until waking suddenly at ten o'clock, they both decide that they had better go to bed. No wonder our families are so frequently disjointed! We do not work together. We do not play together. We do not read together. We do not listen together. And many times we do not even eat together. Home is the place which father has to support and mother maintain. Home is the place where the children are coerced into conduct which they loathe. It is an institution to which father is chained by the vows he once took, and mother is chained by the need for her services, and the children are chained because they have to get their food and shelter somewhere. It is a prison. It is a jail.

And then in the third place, the family needs prayer. Not memorized prayers which someone else has written. Not read prayers. Not silent prayers. Not the repetition of the Lord's Prayer. Spontaneous prayers, in the sense that they come from your own mind and your own heart. Honest prayers in the sense that they represent your deepest yearnings for yourself and for the other members of the family. Spoken prayers in the sense that each member of the family takes his turn at leading the others in a prayer of his own devising. Devotional booklets can be a weapon of the devil; for they can be used to spare the individual the need to face his God with nothing to protect him. The Lord's Prayer itself can be made a shield whereby the timid soul can hold at bay the God who tries to come to him. Whenever every man does that which is right in his own eyes, there is chaos; and even as the many states of this nation had to find their separate fulfillment in allegiance to the one inclusive union, so will there be no real salvation for a human family until each member of it owns allegiance to a power higher than himself. And the seal of that allegiance is spoken prayer to God, so that in the family circle each member bears open witness to the fact that he too is under Gods dominion, asks for God's help, needs God's forgiveness, depends on God's love. It is the goal of any family really worthy of the name, not so much that its members should learn to depend on one another as that its members should learn to depend on God; and there is no telling what might happen in the families of a church if once a day those families assembled for prayer, and if each member of the family talked to God within the hearing of the other members. For many a cell door would be opened and many a bar be bent.

Here's a Faith for You

Among the letters of Emily Dickinson one is still preserved which she had written to her father. At the top of a blank sheet of paper is written "Dear Father," and at the bottom, "Emily." And in between there is nothing at all. This seems to be the way it always was in that household; for after his death Edward Dickinson's body was brought home from the station, and when the undertaker and his assistant had left, Emily's brother Austin leaned over his father's face and kissed his forehead. "There, Father," he said. "I never dared to do that while you were living."

The life and love are gone from many homes today, and they are cells as jails are cells. But there are other homes, too—homes which are cells as our bodies have cells, homes which are parts of the kingdom of God, homes which welcome Jesus as the unseen Guest at every meal and conversation, homes which live and grow and prosper.

And what kind of cell is your home? Is it a cell in the penological sense? Or is it a cell in the biological sense?

You Are Not Dead
When You Die

HE is a strangely thoughtless man who never asks himself what happens to us when we die. Where is Abraham Lincoln today? George Washington? Martin Luther? The apostle Paul? Socrates? When Charles Dickens died, what really happened to him? What happened to Amos and Confucius, to Pilate and Constantine, to Miles Standish and Rufus Jones? Or that loved one whom you have lately lost? What happened to him when his body collapsed? Where did he go when he left you? Where is he now? And what about ourselves? The likelihood is great that not a single one of us will be living on the earth a hundred years from now. And what will be the truth about us then? Will we still be living somewhere? And if so, where and how?

There is nothing morbid in the asking of these questions.

They are, in fact, among the most important matters any man could ever think about, and in the effort to provide an answer to them I want to climb a tower with you now. I want to have us take a look around the landscape and see if we can understand a little better what this life of ours really is and how it seems from points of vantage higher than the daily round.

So up the stairs we climb until we reach the first window in the walls, and even there one fact is clear about the life beyond the grave: the unknown is far greater than the known. Some things we can discern with certainty approaching knowledge, and other things we can assume by inference. But out against the skyline mountain ranges throw their peaks against our vision, and what we know is made as nothing by the sudden sense of that which lies beyond us. Heaven is a country unexplored by mortal man. The tickets there are one-way tickets, and none has ever come to earth again from wanderings across those mountain ranges. Not even Jesus breaks the silence in the manner that we want. For the most part he does not describe heaven at all: he simply takes it for granted. And anyone who demands that paradise be made an open book before him had better climb no higher on the tower stairs, for he will only waste his time. About the life after death, the unknown is far greater than the known.

So much we see so near the ground, but up we go again; and from the second window in the wall we see the fact that any life after death will be divorced from life in the body we have used while on the earth. Buried, the dead body decays. Burned, it is consumed. And nothing is retained for anyone to use or recognize again. The eyes, the hands, the feet, the stomach—all of them will disappear forever. In any life beyond death we may have a body, but it will not be our present body; and with the passing of the flesh which we have known on earth, there will also be dissolved any bonds which were exclusively dependent on that flesh. "In the resurrection," said Jesus, "they neither marry, nor are given in marriage, but are as the angels of God." Those words, writes Leslie Weatherhead, do not mean that a husband and wife will be no dearer than any other personality but that in the life after death no ties will be binding except ties of the spirit. No mere earthborn tie will have any binding power at all, and "marriages made in hell will not be remade in heaven." For when the body dies, it is dead; and all, too, is dead which could not live without the body, which depended upon the body for its life, which found in the body its only meaning and value.

But we are still far from the top of the tower, and from the third of the clefts in the walls we see the further fact that there is nothing in this disappearance of the body which makes impossible the continued existence of parts of the being which are independent of the body. Because we have known no life which is not incarnate, we do not therefore have the right to assume that such life is impossible; and because the activity of the mind can be correlated with observable changes in the physical brain, we cannot therefore claim that the brain is the source of the mind. For it is at least possible that even as the telephone wires do not create the messages they carry, but only pass them on, so the brain does not produce our thoughts, but only transmits them.

It was a confidence like that which Socrates expressed while talking with his friends before his death. "How do you want us to bury you?" Crito had asked him.

"In any way you wish," Socrates replied. "Only you will have to catch me first and see that I do not slip away from you." And then he turned to the little group of people standing around him. "My friends," he said, "I still cannot make Crito believe that I am the Socrates who now talks with you and argues with you. He thinks that I am the one whom he will soon see lying dead, and so he asks how he should bury me. When I drink the poison, I shall no longer remain here with you but shall hasten away to some blessed region of the happy dead. I do not want Crito to say at the funeral that he is laying out Socrates, or taking Socrates to the grave, or burying him. Be brave, and say instead that you are burying my body."

We are still too near ground to say for sure that Socrates was right, but we are high enough to know that such a possibility at least exists. What we call death may be nothing more than "the body becoming incapable of longer serving as the earthly place of the spirit," and no knowledge man now has can make that faith a thing of foolishness. It is a live possibility. It could be true.

So up we go again, and from the fourth of the windows it becomes apparent that any immortality worthy of the name must be a personal immortality. The essential "you" must live on beyond the grave in such a form that you are conscious of being the same person when out of the body as you were while in the body. The reabsorption of your soul into some great cosmic pool of energy would not be life but death, and living on only in the hearts of those who love you would be a ghostly kind of life, diminishing as those who love you diminished, and dying at last as they died. If Lincoln is alive today only in the influence which he has had upon this nation which he loved, his influence is still a precious heritage, but Lincoln himself is dead. If Jesus Christ lives on in nothing but the gospel records of his life, those are still a treasure past all price, but Jesus Christ himself is dead. Either we really live on after death, or we do not; and if we do, then our personalities are not destroyed. They retain their integrity. They hold on to their attributes. They can be identified. They can be recognized.

But thus far we have seen no more than possibilities, and climbing now to look out from the fifth window in the wall, we feel a thrill of hope in finding something surer. For here we see that faith in immortality is a necessary part of faith in God. Deny that God exists, and you have nothing left to tip the scales toward life eternal; but keep your faith in God as Jesus Christ revealed him, and immortality becomes almost a fact beyond dispute. God is great and God is good. He is the maker of all that is made and the planner of all that is planned. In the beginning he made man in his own image, and through the centuries of earth's existence he has brooded over man with love and lovingkindness. Into man's heart God has injected hungers which the earth alone can never satisfy, and on the earth man has been exposed to dangers with which he cannot always cope. Lives are cut short on the earth. Good people fail, and bad people prosper. Little children are born with crippling deformities, and old men face death with the knowledge that they have not lived a quarter of the lives which they were meant to live. "Death at any age is dying young." It is dying with your life unfulfilled, unjustified, unredeemed, and placing side by side in your mind the tragedies of earth and the Christlike God, you have no choice but immortality. For not even an earthly father would set before his hungry children a banquet of surpassing delight and then eat the meal himself while they starved to death for want of it. If God exists at all, there is a life beyond the grave. If God is eternal, we are eternal, too.

We are nearing the top of the tower now, and here before the next window on the way there seems to be a shadow on the ground beneath us. Immortality is not simply sweetness and light, it appears to be saying. Whether everyone eventually "gets to heaven" I do not know. Perhaps we can kill our souls as we can our bodies. Perhaps we can be as stubborn after death as we have been before, and nothing in the way God treats us on the earth implies that God will make us live in heaven if we insist that we would rather live in hell.

For hell still has a meaning for the modern world and one which many Protestants had better think about before they make their homes in it. Some things hell does not mean in a world which God controls. Hell is not an endless condition; for not even an earthly parent of only ordinary goodness would thrash his child for the rest of his life in punishment for rebellion confined to a part of his life. Hell is not God's revenge, not God's purposeless torture of a man who can no longer get away from him; for if God is Christlike, he is not a God of vengeance, not a God of rancor. Nor is hell a torment of flame; for fire has no power except in the world of the flesh, and when the body dies, the threat of fire also dies. But because the old idea of hell has many weak spots in it, there is no reason therefore to discard the whole conception altogether.

This, writes Georgia Harkness, is what the idea really stands for:

(1) That it makes a difference whether or not we accept salvation through the mercy of God; (2) that if we do not repent and turn from our sin, we must suffer the consequences; (3) that there comes a time when we have sinned away the freedom we once had; and (4) that in hell we have cut ourselves off from awareness of the presence of God. . . . What is

so clearly true of this life may well be true of the next. As heaven begins but does not end with the life on earth, so the warping and crippling of human spirits through sin probably is not ended with death. "Whatsoever a man soweth, that shall he also reap"—in this life or the next.[1]

It is a sobering view which we have from this window in the walls of the tower, but it brings to us a truth we badly need. We are playing for keeps in this life of ours, and the manner of our living has abiding consequences. It makes a difference how we live on the earth. It makes an everlasting difference.

From here the climb is but a short one to reach the tower's top, and looking out to far horizons now, we see that if there can be growth toward hurt and pain beyond the grave, so can growth be toward assurance and understanding and joy. This is the state to which we give the name of heaven, and it is the will of God that all who pass beyond the bounds of earth should find their places here, not in hell.

And what is heaven like? We have no photographs, of course, nor can we even paint its picture, but there is a door to understanding in that anonymous "Letter to Saint Peter," which appears on the wall of an American military cemetery in England:

Let them in, Peter, they are very tired;
Give them the couches where the angels sleep.

[1] *Understanding the Christian Faith*, pp. 147-48.

You Are Not Dead When You Die

Let them wake whole again to new dawns fired
With sun, not war. And may their peace be deep.
Remember where the broken bodies lie. . . .
God knows how young they were to die!
Give swing bands, not gold harps, to these our boys.
Let them love, Peter—they have had no time—
Girls sweet as meadow wind, with flowering hair. . . .
They should have trees and bird-song, hills to climb,
The taste of summer in a ripened pear.
Let them in, dear Peter, they are ours.[2]

Any attempt to paint a verbal picture of the life after death runs the twin dangers of letting the imagination get out of hand and of introducing very earthy factors into the description. The "Letter to Saint Peter" does not wholly avoid either one of those perils, but still it points the way toward aspects of the life eternal which no Christian needs to count too good to be true. "It is not inconsistent with what we know of God through Christ to believe that in the life beyond there will be continuance of the individual soul, fellowship with those we love, a lifting of earthly chains of pain and suffering, a chance to grow in the things of Christ, the glory of God's nearer presence." For those who have loved God and tried to serve him there will be joy in heaven. There will be contentment and peace and assurance. There will be deeds to be done and comradeship in doing them. There will be loads to be lifted and strength

[2] According to the *New York Times Book Review*, December 26, 1948.

for the lifting of them. For the life beyond the grave will not be so much the reward of goodness as the experience of goodness, the practice of goodness, the enjoyment of goodness.

And so the sting of death is gone for Christian people, and the grave has lost its victory. For they can face their going from the earth like one who said: "Do I mind dying? Of course, not. People who are fond of me will be sad, but that's all that bothers me. I love life, but I am so curious to see what goes on afterward that sometimes, honestly, I can hardly wait." Or like Henry Ward Beecher, who wrote:

Death is the Christian's vacation morning. School is out. It is time to go home. It is surprising that one should wish life here, who may have life in heaven. And when friends have gone out from us joyously, I think we should go with them to the grave, not singing mournful psalms, but scattering flowers. Christians are wont to walk in black and sprinkle the ground with tears at the very time when they should walk in white and illumine the way by smiles and radiant hope.

A cemetery is not commonly thought to be a place of comfort or encouragement. It is a gloomy spot, we say, and of all of the places to be at midnight, a cemetery would doubtless rank among the least desired. But it should not be so, and while driving past one, I often find myself uplifted, heartened, assured. Death seems often so lonely, so forbidding, so final; but from the cemetery every tombstone seems to be a call across the great divide. "Take heart!" it cries. "We have tasted death. All the host of people represented here have gone through that door which one day waits for you. We have seen and we have known, and from the other side of that experience we say to you that you have no need for fear. You have need only for joy."